Inkscape
Beginner's Guide

Create attractive layout designs, logos, brochures, icons, and more using the Inkscape vector graphics editor

Bethany Hiitola

BIRMINGHAM - MUMBAI

Inkscape
Beginner's Guide

First published: May 2012

Production Reference: 1170512

Published by Packt Publishing Ltd.
Livery Place
35 Livery Street
Birmingham B3 2PB, UK.

ISBN 978-1-84951-720-1

www.packtpub.com

Cover Image by Asher Wishkerman (a.wishkerman@mpic.de)

Credits

Author

Bethany Hiitola

Reviewers

Mark Bystry

Jose Olarte III

Richard Querin

Sylvia Slokker

Acquisition Editor

Sarah Cullington

Lead Technical Editor

Hithesh Uchil

Technical Editors

Ankita Shashi

Manali Mehta

Manasi Poonthottam

Copy Editors

Leonard D'Silva

Laxmi Subramanian

Project Coordinator

Joel Goveya

Proofreader

Chris Brown

Indexer

Monica Ajmera Mehta

Graphics

Manu Joseph

Valentina D'Souza

Production Coordinator

Melwyn D'Sa

Cover Work

Melwyn D'Sa

About the Author

Bethany Hiitola is a working writer. She has worked as a technical writer and multimedia developer for over 12 years. She spends the rest of her time as a wife, mother, and caretaker to pets. She has written more user manuals than she can count, essays, short stories, academic papers, press releases, and feature articles. More details about her writing and life are at her website: www.bethanyhiitola.com

Without you Matt, this book wouldn't have been possible. You are my everything.

About the Reviewers

Mark Bystry is a design engineer by trade. He is also an open source software enthusiast with a penchant for graphic art. Drawing and illustration, 3D modeling, desktop publishing, photography, and videography are just a few of his many interests. Those things also spill into his daily work duties. Mark has come to rely on Inkscape as well as several other leading open source applications to achieve a full range of graphic tasks.

Several years ago Mark teamed up with his online pal, Richard Querin, when they recognized a void within the Inkscape user community, specifically the lack of educational information dedicated to the use of Inkscape. Their vision was of a series of instructional videos geared towards beginners.

Since that time Richard and Mark have made over one hundred videos demonstrating various functions within the application. Though their video series has tapered off, mainly due to their insatiable need to explore all that the technological world has to offer, they still remain avid users of Inkscape and continue to guide novice users in the achievement of their goals.

Jose Olarte III is a graphic designer and photographer from Baguio City, Philippines. He specializes in: user interface design for web, mobile and desktop platforms; print design for magazines and other publications; logo and icon design. When he's not busy pushing pixels and stretching ems, he gets his social fix by tweeting away his thoughts: `twitter.com/brownspank`

> I would like to thank my wife Vanessa for putting up with my extended hours and sharing my passion for work, without which I wouldn't have the strength and motivation to move forward with my creative endeavors.

Richard Querin is a practicing structural engineer with a passion for graphic design, photography, and other creative pursuits. He has contributed graphic design work to several different free and open source projects including websites, mobile and desktop applications, conference graphics, and print advertisements. He has also done numerous Inkscape video tutorials as a co-contributor to the `screencasters.heathenx.org` website.

I would like to thank my family for putting up with my creative antics and providing me the time and space to take on creative pursuits such as these. Thanks also go to my friend and Inkscape compatriot Mark Bystry for his help throughout the years and to Joel Goveya for his patience when it came to getting my reviews back. And finally, a special thanks to my wonderful daughter Emily for making fatherhood an absolute delight.

Sylvia Slokker is a graphics freelancer and IT professional. She started her career in web design and development in 2001, abandoning the career path of process engineer after almost 10 years.

Sylvia moved continents to chase a dream and currently works as a web developer in Australia. She has been creating vector designs since 1994, using both commercial as well as open source software. Nowadays, she uses Inkscape almost exclusively for all her vector work. Sylvia writes tutorials for the web under the nickname Syllie and runs: `verysimpledesigns.com` as a tutorial site for the novice Inkscape artist.

www.PacktPub.com

Support files, eBooks, discount offers and more

You might want to visit www.PacktPub.com for support files and downloads related to your book.

Did you know that Packt offers eBook versions of every book published, with PDF and ePub files available? You can upgrade to the eBook version at www.PacktPub.com and as a print book customer, you are entitled to a discount on the eBook copy. Get in touch with us at service@packtpub.com for more details.

At www.PacktPub.com, you can also read a collection of free technical articles, sign up for a range of free newsletters and receive exclusive discounts and offers on Packt books and eBooks.

http://PacktLib.PacktPub.com

Do you need instant solutions to your IT questions? PacktLib is Packt's online digital book library. Here, you can access, read and search across Packt's entire library of books.

Why Subscribe?

- ◆ Fully searchable across every book published by Packt
- ◆ Copy and paste, print and bookmark content
- ◆ On demand and accessible via web browser

Free Access for Packt account holders

If you have an account with Packt at www.PacktPub.com, you can use this to access PacktLib today and view nine entirely free books. Simply use your login credentials for immediate access.

Table of Contents

Preface **1**

Chapter 1: Getting Started with Vector Graphics **7**

What are vector graphics? **8**

Programs that use vector graphics 8

Vector formats 9

Scalable Vector Graphics **9**

Advantages of an open-standard vector format 10

Additional advantages of SVG vector images over proprietary formats 10

Disadvantages of vector graphics over non-vector formats 11

Determining when to use vector or rasterized graphics **11**

Time for action – basic design **12**

Time for action – vector versus rasterized images **13**

Time for action – building brochure files **14**

Summary **16**

Chapter 2: Installing and Opening Inkscape **17**

Inkscape's features **17**

Installing Inkscape **18**

Time for action – downloading Inkscape **19**

Troubleshooting installation **20**

The basics of the software **21**

Time for action – getting started with Inkscape **22**

Understanding a new document **28**

Time for action – learning more about the main screen **28**

Summary **34**

Chapter 3: How to Manage Files **35**

Creating new files **35**

Using predefined-sized document dimensions 36

Time for action – creating a new CD cover	**37**
Custom document dimensions	**39**
Time for action – creating a new custom file size for a postcard	**39**
Saving Inkscape files	**44**
Saving in Inkscape SVG	44
Time for action – saving an Inkscape SVG	**45**
Exporting files	47
Time for action – exporting to PNG	**47**
Creating a customized default document	**49**
Time for action – creating a new default document	**50**
How to structure project files	**51**
Managing multiple file projects	52
Time for action – exporting a batch of images	**52**
Renaming object IDs	54
Importing non-native Inkscape files	**55**
Time for action – importing a PDF into Inkscape	**56**
Embedding and linking image files	**58**
Embedding files in Inkscape	59
Time for action – embedding a logo into your design	**59**
Linking external files in Inkscape	61
Time for action – linking a photograph into a brochure design	**61**
Summary	**63**
Chapter 4: Creating your First Graphics	**65**
Paths	**65**
Creating your first vector graphic	**67**
Creating a polygon	67
Time for action – opening a new document	**67**
Time for action – creating a star	**69**
Time for action – saving your graphic	**72**
Creating ellipses and arcs	74
Time for action – creating the Ellipse	**74**
Time for action – making an arc	**75**
Complex Shapes	78
Time for action – combining shapes	**78**
Freehand objects (Paths)	82
Time for action – creating a freehand object	**82**
Using grids and guidelines	**84**
Time for action – viewing the Grid	**84**
Time for action – making guides	**87**
Summary	**88**

Chapter 5: How to Work with Layers	**89**
Defining layers and how to create them	90
Time for action – creating a layer	91
Using Layers in an example drawing	93
Time for action – using Layers in web design	93
Locking layers	98
Time for action – locking a layer	98
Hiding layers	99
Time for action – hiding layers	100
Duplicating layers	104
Time for action – duplicating layers	104
Arranging layers	105
Time for action – moving layers	105
Time for action – nesting layers	108
Renaming layers	109
Time for action – renaming a layer	109
Deleting layers	110
Time for action – deleting a layer	110
Blend mode	112
Time for action – using Blend mode	112
Summary	114
Chapter 6: Building Objects	**115**
Working with objects	115
Time for action – creating a simple object	116
Fill and Stroke	121
Fill and Stroke dialog	121
Time for action – using the Fill and Stroke dialog	121
Color palette bar	126
Time for action – using the color palette	126
Dropper	127
Time for action – using the dropper tool	128
Grouping	129
Time for action – grouping objects	129
Clipping and masking	133
Time for action – clipping objects	133
Time for action – masking objects	142
Summary	144

Chapter 7: Using Paths   **145**
  Working with paths   **145**
  Time for action – using the Bezier tool   **146**
  Transforming objects into paths   **155**
    Stroke to paths   155
  Time for action – creating spiros and swirls   **155**
    Object to Path   163
  Time for action – Object to Path   **164**
  Path options   **166**
  Time for action – creating an icon   **167**
  Summary   **170**

Chapter 8: How to Style Text   **171**
  Text and Font editor   **171**
  Time for action – opening and using the Text and Font editor   **172**
    Kerning   173
  Time for action – kerning text   **174**
    Text styling keyboard shortcuts   176
  Using paths and text   **177**
  Time for action – using a path for text   **177**
    Placing text within a closed shape   179
  Time for action – placing text in a closed shape   **180**
  Spell check and find/replace   **181**
  Time for action – performing a find and replace   **182**
  Text effects   **182**
  Time for action – using text effects   **183**
  Creating text reflections   **184**
  Time for action – creating a reflection   **185**
  Summary   **189**

Chapter 9: Using Filters   **191**
  What are filters?   **191**
  Using the Filter editor   **192**
  Time for action – using filters   **193**
  Using filters with text   **197**
  Time for action – using filters with text   **197**
  Images and effects   **198**
  Time for action – using filters with images   **199**
  Tracing images   **201**
  Time for action – using Potrace   **202**
  Time for action – using SIOX   **205**
  Summary   **207**

Chapter 10: Extensions in Inkscape	**209**
Templates	**210**
Installing and using new templates	210
Time for action – installing Inkscape templates	**211**
Creating your own custom templates	212
Time for action – modifying an existing Inkscape template	**212**
Time for action – creating a custom template	**213**
What are extensions?	**213**
Examples of extension tutorials	214
Installation extensions	**215**
Summary	**215**
Chapter 11: Working with Images	**217**
Importing from the Open Clip Art Library (Linux and Mac users)	217
Time for action – using the Open Clip Art Library (Mac users only)	**218**
Basics about photo manipulation	**219**
Time for action – blurring the background of a photograph	**220**
Converting raster logos to vector-based logos	**228**
Time for action – converting a logo to a vector-based image	**228**
Summary	**229**
Chapter 12: Using the XML Editor	**231**
Inkscape's XML Editor	**231**
Time for action – accessing the XML Editor	**232**
XML Editor basics	**234**
SVG basics	**237**
Attribute types	237
Basic attributes	238
Paths	239
Shapes	239
Images	245
Text	245
Using the XML Editor to change characteristics	**246**
Time for action – using the XML Editor to change object characteristics	**246**
Using XML and graphics with programmers	**248**
Summary	**248**
Appendix A: Where to Find More Information	**249**
Official sites	**249**
Articles and tutorials	**249**
Community	**250**
Blogs	**250**
Twitter	**251**

Appendix B: Keyboard Shortcuts   **253**

Appendix C: Glossary of Terms   **257**

Appendix D: Pop Quiz Answers   **261**

Index   **269**

Preface

Are you ready to jump into the world of graphic design and illustration? Or have you just begun to explore new tools that can broaden your skill set in these specialties? *Inkscape Beginner's Guide* is the perfect book to start this journey into the world of vector graphics. This book starts at the very basics of a complex, open source tool on the market today – Inkscape 0.48 (current version as of the publication of this book). Learn everything you need to know from setting up a document file to completing your first illustration.

The Inkscape graphics editor can be daunting when just learning the tool. There are so many features one may not know where to start. *Inkscape Beginner's Guide* can help to alleviate these fears; it takes a simple step-by-step approach to learning the software. It starts at the very beginning, unlocking the secret to the software's interface, explaining menus and the overall areas of the user interface, and then jumps into real projects that illustrate some simple graphic-building concepts.

Expect to learn everything from using paths, text styles, filters, and images—while building a brochure, logo, icons, illustration, and more—all in the context of real graphic design, illustration, or web projects. Using an informative but simple approach, learning Inkscape becomes a fun and interactive process.

Welcome to the world of Inkscape 0.48 and vector graphics! This book is an informational step-by-step beginner's book for someone just starting their journey in using Inkscape 0.48 in the creation of vector graphics. No previous experience using Inkscape 0.48 or other previous vector graphics programs are required. The book will be chalked full of real-world examples, detailed step-by-step instructions and associated screen captures to keep the information approachable yet easy to digest—and don't forget fun!

What this book covers

Chapter 1, Getting Started with Vector Graphics, starts before Inkscape, at the beginning of vector graphics. We begin by defining vector graphics and how they are used online and within print projects. Then we start digging into Inkcape learning about how the program began and how it fits in the world of vector graphics today.

Chapter 2, Installing and Opening Inkscape, discusses where to download Inkscape 0.48, the most recent version of the software and its unique features, as well as detailed descriptions about how to install the software. Included in this are screen captures that define the main areas of the program and menu items—all of which is very helpful when opening the software for the first time.

Chapter 3, How to Manage Files, is all about files and managing them. Inkscape can import a number of file formats and then edit them. Then, after completing a project Inkscape has the ability to save and export graphics in a number of formats. We will discuss all of these options as well as the native Inkscape SVG format and the benefits of using project folders.

Chapter 4, Creating your First Graphics, starts by defining paths and shapes, a basis for all projects going forward in Inkscape. Then it focuses on creating your very first Inkscape object – a star. Also discussed in this chapter are ellipses, complex shapes, freehand object, grids, and guidelines.

Chapter 5, How to Work with Layers, is all about layers in Inkscape. You will learn the basics like how to create new layers, delete, arrange, and blend layers, as well as hiding and duplicating layers, all the while working on a sample blog header project.

Chapter 6, Building Objects, helps you learn about objects and how Inkscape interprets them, how to change object features, change fill and stroke, grouping objects, combining objects, and how to best use the masking and clipping features.

Chapter 7, Using Paths focuses, on using paths. Again we start with the basics: defining paths, how to work with them in Inkscape, transforming, combining, and placing paths. The bulk of this chapter will focus on an illustration project that will assist you in learning all you need to know about paths.

Chapter 8, How to Style Text, teaches how you can manipulate and style text for any design. It is a practical chapter that covers using paths and text to create visual appeal, text and frames, the basics like spellcheck and find/replace, text effects, and a simple project to show how to create a text reflection.

Chapter 9, Using Filters, focuses on using filters with text and images to give a further dimension to your vector graphics. Projects will focus on using images and text—including a detailed example with step-by-step instructions on using filters with text.

Chapter 10, Extensions in Inkscape, is as expected, about extensions or templates and plugins that can assist in the design process for vector graphics. You will learn how to install templates, extensions, and about the availability of certain extension or scripts that might be useful.

Chapter 11, Working with Images, is all about importing photographs or images into Inkscape and manipulating them. Specifically, you will be working on a few sample projects that deal with photographs and filters.

Chapter 12, Using the XML Editor, teaches you about the XML editor that is included within Inkscape. It covers the basic XML structure tree, as well as how you can manipulate this code to change objects in your projects.

Appendix A, Where to Find More Information, provides web links to people and places that can help you learn even more about Inkscape.

Appendix B, Keyboard Shortcuts, mentions the basic keyboard shortcuts for Inkscape 0.48.

Appendix C, Glossary of Terms, is a glossary of Inkscape and basic design terms used throughout the book.

What you need for this book

You'll need the latest version of Inkscape 0.48 and Internet access (to download some example clip art and projects).

If you are using a Mac, then you may also need the X11 app on your system to run Inkscape (this typically comes pre-installed on Leopard OSX).

Who this book is for

This book is intended for novice graphic and web designers who want to expand their graphic software expertise. General familiarity with a graphics program is recommended, but not required.

Conventions

In this book, you will find several headings appearing frequently.

To give clear instructions of how to complete a procedure or task, we use:

Time for action – heading

1. Action 1
2. Action 2
3. Action 3

Instructions often need some extra explanation so that they make sense, so they are followed with:

What just happened?

This heading explains the working of tasks or instructions that you have just completed.

You will also find some other learning aids in the book, including:

Pop quiz – heading

These are short multiple-choice questions intended to help you test your own understanding.

Have a go hero – heading

This sets practical challenges and gives you ideas for experimenting with what you have learned.

You will also find a number of styles of text that distinguish between different kinds of information. Here are some examples of these styles, and an explanation of their meaning.

Code words in text are shown as follows: "Find the Inkscape icon in the `Application` or `Programs` folder"

New terms and important words are shown in bold. Words that you see on the screen, in menus or dialog boxes for example, appear in the text like this: "Open Inkscape, and from the main menu, select **File | New | CD_cover_300dpi**.".

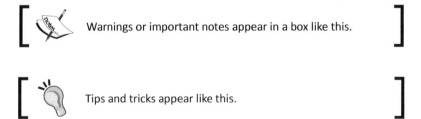

Warnings or important notes appear in a box like this.

Tips and tricks appear like this.

Reader feedback

Feedback from our readers is always welcome. Let us know what you think about this book—what you liked or may have disliked. Reader feedback is important for us to develop titles that you really get the most out of.

To send us general feedback, simply send an e-mail to `feedback@packtpub.com`, and mention the book title in the subject of your message.

If there is a topic that you have expertise in and you are interested in either writing or contributing to a book, see our author guide on `www.packtpub.com/authors`.

Customer support

Now that you are the proud owner of a Packt book, we have a number of things to help you to get the most from your purchase.

Downloading the color images of this book

We also provide you a PDF fifile that has color images of the screenshots used in this book. The color images will help you better understand the changes in the output. You can download this file from `http://www.packtpub.com/sites/default/files/downloads/images.pdf`

Errata

Although we have taken every care to ensure the accuracy of our content, mistakes do happen. If you find a mistake in one of our books—maybe a mistake in the text or the code—we would be grateful if you would report this to us. By doing so, you can save other readers from frustration and help us improve subsequent versions of this book. If you find any errata, please report them by visiting `http://www.packtpub.com/support`, selecting your book, clicking on the **errata submission form** link, and entering the details of your errata. Once your errata are verified, your submission will be accepted and the errata will be uploaded to our website, or added to any list of existing errata, under the Errata section of that title.

Piracy

Piracy of copyright material on the Internet is an ongoing problem across all media. At Packt, we take the protection of our copyright and licenses very seriously. If you come across any illegal copies of our works, in any form, on the Internet, please provide us with the location address or website name immediately so that we can pursue a remedy.

Please contact us at `copyright@packtpub.com` with a link to the suspected pirated material.

We appreciate your help in protecting our authors, and our ability to bring you valuable content.

Questions

You can contact us at `questions@packtpub.com` if you are having a problem with any aspect of the book, and we will do our best to address it.

1

Getting Started with Vector Graphics

Inkscape *is an open source, free program that creates vector-based graphics that can be used in web and print design, in interface and logo creation, and in material cutting. Its capabilities are similar to those of commercial products such as* **Adobe Illustrator**, **Macromedia Freehand**, *and* **CorelDraw** *and can be used for any number of practical purposes—creating vector graphics for use in illustrations, business letterheads, computer and electronic wallpapers, and designing web pages and the elements within them.*

This is a beginner's guide to using Inkscape. This means you will learn all the ins and outs of using this software—including all the details about the interface, menus, buttons, as well as how to create graphics. We'll start with the very basic parts of graphics and build up as we continue through the book to more complex graphics projects pointing out how you would use these items in everyday projects.

However, before learning the details on how to use Inkscape, let's take a step back and define vector graphics, how a computer displays them, how vector graphics work together, and why we want to use them in design.

Specifically, this chapter will teach you the following:

- ◆ What vector graphics are
- ◆ Scalable Vector Graphics and Inkscape
- ◆ Reasons for using vector graphics over rasterized images
- ◆ How vector graphics are used in design

Let's get started!

What are vector graphics?

A **vector graphic** is made up of points, lines, curves, and shapes or polygons, which are all based on mathematical equations. Inkscape uses these objects and can convert them into paths. A path is a line with a start and end, which are also calculated with a mathematical equation. These paths are not limited to being straight—they can be of any shape, size, and even encompass any number of curves. When you combine them, they create drawings, diagrams, and can even help create certain fonts.

How does this all relate to vector-based graphics? Vector-based graphics aren't made up of pixels. Since they are resolution-independent, you can make them larger (by scaling) and the image quality will stay the same, lines and edges stay clean, and the same images can be used on items as small as letterheads or business cards, blown up to be billboards, or used in high-definition animation sequences. This flexibility, often accompanied by smaller file sizes, makes vector graphics ideal—especially in the world of Internet, computer displays of varying resolution, and hosting services for web pages. Inkscape can help in the navigation of those waters of vector graphics and is a tool that can be invaluable when designing for the digital world as well as print.

These characteristics make vector graphics very different from JPEGs, GIFs, or BMP images—all of which are considered raster or bitmap images, made up of tiny squares called pixels or bits. If you magnify these images, you will see that they are made up of a grid (or bitmap), and if magnified further, they will become blurry and grainy as each pixel with bitmap square's zoom level grows larger.

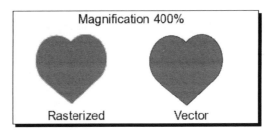

Programs that use vector graphics

As stated earlier in the chapter, many programs and applications are similar to Inkscape and can open vector graphics. Some can only open these files for viewing purposes and others can edit them.

Other applications typically used for page layout, but which can open and manipulate vector graphics include **Scribus**, **Quark Xpress**, and **Adobe InDesign**. Scribus is unique in that it is also open source (as Inkscape is) and can even import SVG files (the file type Inkscape uses) and manipulate them. The other programs can open, import, place, scale, and distort `.eps files`, a vector graphic file type, but unfortunately cannot create or otherwise modify vector graphics.

To create vector graphics, you will use illustration programs like Inkscape—which this book is about—or other programs like **Adobe Illustrator**, **Adobe Freehand Corel Draw**, **Freehand**, **XARA Xtreme**, or **Serif DrawPlus**. These programs all have native file formats, but allow you to export your graphics as `.eps` or `.svg` files, as needed. What is different about these applications than those for page layout is that you start with a completely blank document that allows you to fully design or draw what you would like, whereas the page layout application focuses on full page layouts.

Vector formats

In the previous section, it was noted that `.eps`, an **Encapsulated Post Script** file, is a common vector graphic format—or open format—that can be read by most applications that open and/or create vector graphics. However, there are other file formats that are also considered vector-graphic compatible. These include Inkscape's `.svg` format, Adobe Illustrator (`.ai`), Adobe Freehand (`.Fhx`), and Adobe Flash files, which are mostly vector data and are considered proprietary formats, tied more directly to the prospective software that can open them.

There are a number of other proprietary graphic file formats which can include vector graphics within them as well as rasterized (or bitmap) graphics. These include:

- **Adobe Photoshop** (`.psd`): This includes vector layers such as text, shapes, and paths
- **Adobe Acrobat Portable Document Format** (`.pdf`): This contains vector data and bitmap images in different forms
- The **Encapsulated Post Script** file (`.eps`): This, again, can hold both vector data and bitmap images

Also note that `.eps` files are basically the same files a Post Script laser printer uses. Both file types are developed by Adobe and are the foundation of the Adobe PDF format.

Scalable Vector Graphics

What does Inkscape use? A completely different file format—one that is fairly complex in nature, but works well for the flexible nature of vector graphics. They can be edited within Inkscape and can be opened in a text editor and edited at an XML code level. Inkscape uses **Scalable Vector Graphics** (SVG), a vector-based drawing format that incorporates some basic principles:

- A drawing can (and should) be scalable to any size without losing detail
- A drawing can use an unlimited number of smaller drawings used in any number of ways (and reused) and still be a part of a larger whole

More specifically, Scalable Vector Graphics (SVG) is an XML-based file format for describing two-dimensional vector graphics. The specification defines an open standard that has been in development with the World Wide Web Consortium (W3C) since 1999.

Inkscape was built with SVG and the W3C web standards in mind, which give it a number of features, including a rich body of XML (Extensible Markup Language) with complete descriptions. Inkscape drawings can be reused in other SVG-compliant drawing programs and can adapt to different presentation methods. The .svg format has growing support across most web browsers (Firefox, Chrome, Opera, Safari, Internet Explorer).

The SVG files then, which are inherently XML, can be searched, indexed, scripted, and compressed within a text editor. In fact, they can be created and edited with a text editor if required, but drawing programs like Inkscape can create the SVG files. In fact, Inkscape has an XML editor feature which allows direct edits to the XML files; more information on this is in *Chapter 12*, *How you can use the XML Editor*.

Advantages of an open-standard vector format

There are some slight differences between traditional vector graphics and SVG. All vector graphics are scalable, use smaller-sized files, and have the flexibility to be resized when needed. However, the vector graphic format of SVG has even more detailed advantages than the vector graphic native.

Additional advantages of SVG vector images over proprietary formats

SVG vector images, because they are based on XML, have some distinct advantages over open standard vector formats. These are as follows:

- They can be read and modified by a large range of tools (including browsers, text editors, and other vector graphics software, as described previously)
- They are smaller and more compressible than JPEG and GIF images which are often used in web design
- They are also scalable, like vector graphics
- Text in SVG can be searched, edited, indexed, and more
- SVG is an open-standard
- SVG files are pure XML, which allows them to be opened in other programs (or even a text editor) and edited in non-graphical UI ways (or by programmers directly)
- Most modern browsers offer some support for SVG. Internet Explorer 8, however, does not offer this support

There are still some limitations in the Inkscape program, even though it aims to be fully SVG-compliant. For example, as of version 0.48, it still does not support animation or use SVG fonts within the software for design—though there are plans to add these capabilities into future versions.

Disadvantages of vector graphics over non-vector formats

The biggest drawback to vector graphic formats is that they are not ideally suited to working with photographs. Sure, Inkscape and other vector graphic applications can open, import, or place photographs into projects, but the colors and complexities of displaying the photograph will essentially overwhelm the application. Also, as stated earlier, as photographs are very much rasterized images being imported into the vector-based application, once you re-size or scale the photograph, the integrity of the photograph can be lost.

This same complexity will appear for advanced coloring and lighting effects when using vector graphics as well—the more you try to make it look like a photograph, the more you might need to rasterize part of the vector graphic as well, essentially making it a non-vector graphic.

Another known drawback for vector graphics is interoperability. If you want to share files between vector graphic applications, you might run into some issues, even when you use `.eps` files which are more universally accepted as a vector graphic format. Vector information can be lost during the conversion. All fonts, elements, and objects need to be embedded (not linked) and tested thoroughly—however, this sharing is not impossible and entirely depends on the applications being used. Using Inkscape across teams as the development tool can help solve this problem as the application is open source and free to download.

If you are new to design, you might be surprised to learn that even when you are using a word processing program, you are using vector graphics all the time—fonts! Fonts illustrate two common properties of vector graphics:

- An entire font, with all its letters, numbers, and symbols, has a very small file size
- Fonts can be set to any size without losing quality

Some vector-based applications, including Inkscape, allow you to convert text to paths so you can modify the shapes of the letters themselves.

Determining when to use vector or rasterized graphics

We've spent a lot of time discussing vector graphics and how they differ from rasterized bitmap images. In doing so, it is also important to know when it is best to use each type, because there are instances when it does make sense to use one over the other.

Let's say we're doing a project that will get printed; a brochure—and for best results, we'll use both vector and bitmap graphics. We'll look at the most basic steps of how to put this brochure together in the following section.

Time for action – basic design

For this example, let's look at the design elements and determine how we would put them together in a design:

1. Determine the exact size of the brochure. For our example, we'll focus on creating the outside of an 8.5 x 11 tri-fold brochure. Specifically, the cover design of this brochure is as follows:

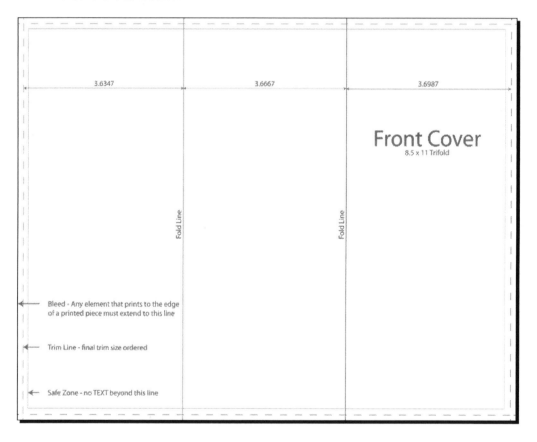

2. Design a basic front cover layout. We'll use the following one for the cover:

3. Decide on the elements we will use for the design. For ours, we'll have a photograph, company logo, brochure title, and some additional copy.

What just happened?

We just did the basic planning required to create a brochure in any graphics program. We determined the physical size of the document, the basic layout, as well as the elements we have available for use in the design.

Time for action – vector versus rasterized images

Now we need to figure out what elements go where and which graphic types will work best. Determine what type of graphics each of our design elements should be to best suit our needs (and the design) and make sure we have the files in that format.

1. Photographs naturally have a lot of colors and gradients, and are often taken in a fixed size from a digital camera. That said, the files are rasterized bitmaps and can be in any number of file formats—including `.tif`, `.jpg`, `.gif`, or `.png`, and are larger in size. Photographs don't lend themselves to being vector graphics.

2. Logos should be portable, so that they can look clean at any size and resolution. The graphics themselves are often simple with less color variation and therefore lend themselves to being vector graphics as opposed to bitmaps. We'll use a graphic-based on one in the `Openclipart.org` collection, which will be explained later, as an example for a company logo. You can use files of the SVG, AI, or EPS format.

3. The company name/title and copy will be text, which is a font and vector graphic. It can still be scaled to accommodate both the boldness of the company name and also be a body copy for the brochure:

What just happened?

We took each piece of the design puzzle and determined the best file types for each element. We collected our files and got them ready for the design phase, which is up next.

Time for action – building brochure files

Take all of the elements we defined—both bitmaps and vector graphics—and create the outside design of the brochure as follows:

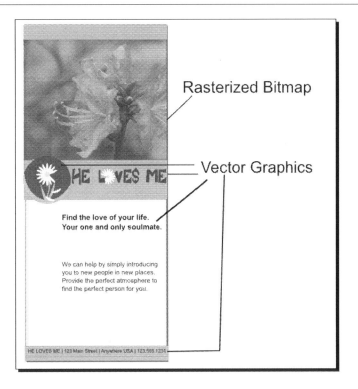

What just happened?

We looked at a full brochure design to determine which elements should be rasterized bitmaps and which should be vector graphics. When done correctly, the graphics seamlessly work together in a design.

Pop quiz – understanding vector graphics

What are the advantages of scalable vector graphics?

a. Smaller file sizes which can be compressed

b. Projects can be printed at any resolution

c. Can be searched, edited, and indexed with a text editor

d. All of the above

Summary

This chapter was dedicated to teaching you the basics about vector graphics and how they differ from bitmap images. We learned how vector graphics are resolution-independent and why we might want to use them in design, how Inkscape supports Scalable Vector Graphics (SVG), which is an open format, and the advantages of using these types of open graphics instead of proprietary. We also took some practical time learning to distinguish when it is best to use vector graphics and when raster images are needed.

Now it is time to learn how to install Inkscape 0.48 and begin creating vector graphics of our own!

2
Installing and Opening Inkscape

To start using Inkscape, you must install it first! This chapter starts by explaining where to download Inkscape from, the most recent version and its features, as well as detailed descriptions about how to install the software. It also includes a brief rundown of the application window and the main areas of where to find items when opening it for the first time.

In this chapter, we will learn:

- ◆ Inkscape 0.48's features
- ◆ Where to download Inkscape
- ◆ How to install Inkscape (Windows, Mac, Linux)
- ◆ Potential troubleshooting items when installing
- ◆ Basics of the Inkscape software
- ◆ Opening your first document

Let's get started and start downloading!

Inkscape's features

Inkscape is a free, open source program developed by a group of volunteers under the **GNU General Public License** (**GPL**). You not only get a free download but can use the program to create items with it and freely distribute them, modify the program itself, and share that modified program with others.

Inkscape uses **Scalable Vector Graphics (SVG)**, a vector-based drawing language, as described in *Chapter 1, Getting Started with Vector Graphics*. The basic principles that apply to SVG graphics apply to Inkscape principles as well:

◆ A drawing can (and should) be scalable to any size without losing detail

◆ A drawing can use an unlimited number of smaller drawings that can be used in any number of ways (and reused) and be a part of a larger whole

The current Inkscape version at the time of this book being printed is 0.48.2.1 and the 0.48.3 version will be available before Inkscape 0.49 is released.

Installing Inkscape

Inkscape is available for download for Windows, Macintosh, Linux, or Solaris operating systems. Before you install Inkscape, you will need to check that you have all of the required elements, listed as follows:

◆ Operating system: Windows XP, Vista, 7, Mac OS X 10.4 Tiger, 10.5 Leopard or 10.6 Snow Leopard, or higher. Most Linux distributions are supported. Note: Windows 98/ME and 2000 are no longer supported.

◆ To run on the Mac OS X operating system, Inkscape typically runs under X11—an implementation of the X Window System software that makes it possible to run X11-based applications in Mac OS X. The X11 application has shipped with the Mac OS X since version 10.5. Snow Leopard requires Apple X11/XQuartz 2.3.4 or higher. Leopard requires Apple X11 2.1.6 or XQuartz. Tiger requires Apple X11 1.1.3.

 When you open Inkscape on a Mac, it will first open X11 and run Inkscape within that program. Loss of some shortcut key options will occur, but all functionality is present using menus and toolbars.

◆ Disk space: A minimum of 190 MB free. More free space is required to store your graphics projects. You can, however, run a portable version of Inkscape on some operating systems (like Windows 7). These installations can run on a portable USB drive and only require 80 MB of space.

◆ Inkscape requires an Internet connection if you plan to use the **Open Clip Art Library**.

 Open Clip Art Library is only available on a Macintosh installation.

Time for action – downloading Inkscape

In a few simple steps, you will be able to download Inkscape 0.48 from the Internet and install it on your computer:

1. Go to the official Inkscape website at `http://www.inkscape.org/` and download the appropriate version of the software for your computer.

2. Double-click the downloaded Inkscape installation package to start the installation.

 For the Mac OS, a DMG file is downloaded. Double-click it and then drag-and-drop the Inkscape package to the `Application` folder. For any Windows device, a `.exe` file is downloaded. Double-click that file to start and and continue to complete the installation. For Linux-based computers, there are a number of distributions available. Be sure to download and install the correct installation package for your system.

3. Find the Inkscape icon in the `Application` or `Programs` folder. It should look like the following icon:

4. If you see this icon, you have a successful installation. Now it is time to open Inkscape for the first time.

5. Double-click the Inkscape icon and the program will automatically open to the main screen.

 If you are using a Macintosh computer, Inkscape opens within the X11 application and may take slightly longer to load.

What just happened?

In a few simple steps, you downloaded the Inkscape installation package and installed it on your system. When Inkscape opens for the first time, you will see the main screen, as shown in the following screenshot, with a new blank document ready to go:

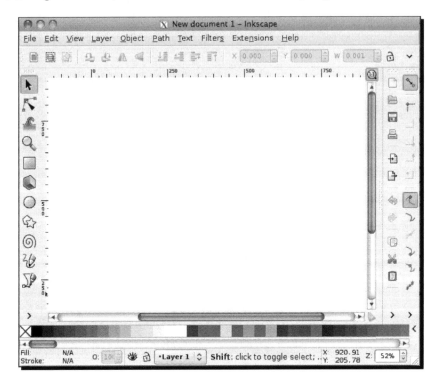

 In this book, the screenshots will be specific to the Mac OS X software. Don't be concerned if this is not your computer operating system of choice; the software itself is very similar between them and notable differences in the Inkscape software screens will be highlighted.

Troubleshooting installation

Installing Inkscape is generally pretty simple to do. However, if you run into any issues, take note of the following tips:

- Make a note of your computer's manufacturer, operating system type, and version and make sure you downloaded the appropriate installation package.

- Also remember once the installation has occurred, the Inkscape icon to launch the software will be in the `Application` or `Programs` folder on your computer

If you are still having issues, there are a number of useful articles, tutorials, forums, and more that can help you in all matters of Inkscape—including installation. Here's the most common and useful one:

- The official **Inkscape Homepage**: `http://inkscape.org/`. It will provide you with all the manuals, current download release information, forums, and every bit of information about Inkscape you want to know.

Other important links from the official homepage are as follows:

- **Manual and documentation**: `http://tavmjong.free.fr/INKSCAPE/MANUAL/html/index.html`
- **Wiki**: `http://wiki.inkscape.org/`
- **Forums**: `http://www.inkscapeforum.com/`
- **Mailing list**: `http://inkscape.org`
- **Blog**: `http://planet.inkscape.org/`
- **For developers**: `https://launchpad.net/inkscape`
- **Clip Art**: `http://www.openclipart.org/`
- **Galleries**: `http://wiki.inkscape.org/wiki/index.php/Galleries`

> From forums to direct installation instructions, `Inkscape.org` is the best place to find information about Inkscape as it compiles all of the latest information about Inkscape from the developers to the users. The mailing lists provide detailed information as well as numerous resources for troubleshooting.

The basics of the software

The Inkscape interface is based on the GNOME UI standard, which uses visual cues and feedback for any icons. For example:

- Hovering your mouse over any icon displays a pop-up description of the icon.
- If an icon has a dark gray border, it is active and can be used.
- If an icon is grayed out, it is not currently available to use with the current selection.
- All icons that are in execution mode (or busy) are covered by a dark shadow. This signifies that the application is busy and won't respond to any edit request.
- There is a Notification region in the status bar on the main screen that displays dynamic help messages. These messages display key shortcuts and basic information on how to use the Inkscape software based on which objects and tools are selected.

Time for action – getting started with Inkscape

In order to feel completely comfortable using the Inkscape software, let's learn the basics of the Inkscape interface. This will include menus, toolbars, and dialog boxes. Let's get started!

Find the Inkscape icon in the `Application` or `Programs` folder and double-click it to open the program.

You will see the main window of the Inkscape software, as follows, with different areas of the screen highlighted. Within the main screen, there is the main menu, command, snap and status bar, tool controls, and a color palette, as shown in the following screenshot:

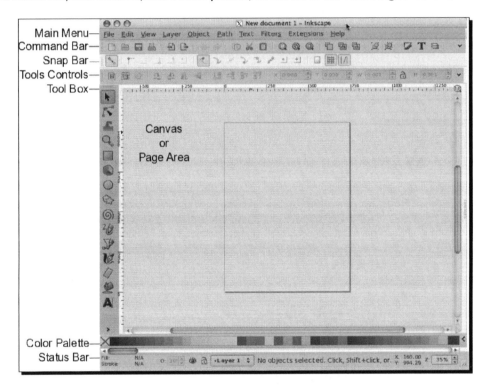

 On some external resources, canvas and page are used almost interchangeably in terms of the Inkscape interface. Technically, however, a canvas is the entire editable area, whereas the page area is the area within the page borders.

1. You will use the main menu frequently when working on your projects. This is the central location to find every tool and menu item in the program—even those found in the visual-based toolbars below it on the screen. When you select a main menu item in Inkscape, you see a menu drop-down with a text description and shortcut key combination for the feature. This can be helpful when first learning the program as it provides you with easier and often faster ways to use the most commonly-used functions of the program.

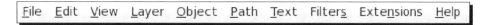

Let's take a general tour of the toolbars seen on this main screen. We'll pay close attention to the tools we'll use most frequently.

2. The command bar toolbar contains the most frequently-used commands in Inkscape.

As seen in the previous image, you can create a new document, open an existing one, save, print, cut, paste, zoom, add text, and much more. Hover your mouse over each icon for details about its function. By default, when you open Inkscape, this toolbar is on the top of the main screen:

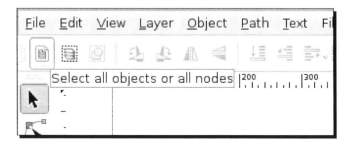

3. Found vertically on the right-hand side of the main screen, the snap bar toolbar is designed to help with the snap to features of Inkscape.

It lets you easily align items (snap to guides), force objects to align to paths (snap to paths), or snap to bounding boxes and edges. More on alignment and snap to bounding boxes will be explained in later chapters of the book when we start building example projects.

The tool controls options change depending on which tool you have selected in the toolbox (described in the next section). When you are creating objects, it provides you with all the detailed options—size, position, angles, and attributes—specific to the tool you are currently using. With the Select tool active, it looks like the following image:

The tool controls bar is located on the top of the main window, just below the command bar.

You have options to select/deselect objects within a layer, rotate or mirror objects, adjust object locations on the canvas and scaling options, and much more. Use it to define object properties when they are selected on the canvas.

4. You'll use the toolbox frequently. It is located on the left-hand side of the screen and contains all of the main tools for creating objects, selecting and modifying objects, and drawing. To select a tool, click the icon. If you double-click a tool, you can see that tool's preferences (and change them).

5. The palette bar of the Inkscape screen controls fill and stroke color options. **Fill** is the color that fills the object or shape. Alternatively, **stroke** is the outline around the object or shape.

Using the palette bar, there are a few ways you can set the fill and stroke in Inkscape:

❏ From the palette bar, click a color and drag it from the palette onto objects to change their fill. If you hold the *Shift* key and drag a color box onto an object, it will set the stroke color.

❏ Select an object on your canvas by clicking it and then right-click a color box in the palette. A pop-up menu appears with options to set the fill and stroke.

❏ Select an object on your canvas and then left-click a color box in the palette to immediately set the fill of an object. Press *Shift* and left-click a color box to immediately set the stroke color.

There are a large number of color boxes to choose from. Use the palette bar scroll bar along the bottom to see more choices to the right of those displaying on the screen. You can also click the small caret at the right end of the toolbar to allow for a greater selection of colors—even customizable color palettes as well.

6. The status bar contains information relating to a selected object within the canvas or page of your document. You can also use it to modify canvas settings:

Here are the details:

❏ **Style Indicator** focuses a bit more on the selected object. If you select any object on your canvas, you can change its fill (overall color of the object) or stroke (border color). Drag a color from the palette to this section for easy color changes. Right-clicking the **Style Indicators** provides a pop-up menu, letting you make quick and easy coloring edits. Double-clicking the

Style Indicators will launch the **Fill & Stroke** dialog box. If you right-click the number next to the **Stroke Style Indicator**, you will get a choice of Stroke thicknesses to choose from.

❑ The **Opacity Setting** is the drop-down box near the **Style Indicators**. Right-click the drop-down box to change the opacity (or transparency) percentage (%) value (the default is **100%**). A pop-up menu displays a set of preset values to choose from. If you left-click the drop-down box, it allows direct entry of a value or a change of the value with the up/down arrows.

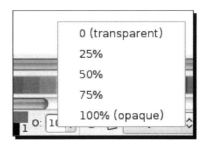

❑ **Layer information**: Within Inkscape, when you create documents, you can have many layers of objects. This gives great flexibility when creating graphics of any kind. You can move groups of objects at once (placing a group of them on a layer) and separate objects by layer to manipulate and affect how they interact with one another when stacked, re-ordered, or hidden. You can also set certain settings by layer. You can even create drafts or different versions of mockups and keep all of this in one file.

❑ The layer information lets you choose which layer you are currently using and placing objects to—this is called the **drawing layer**. You can then set whether this layer is visible or locked. Sometimes you can use your documents as a **working draft** and decide to hide certain layers while developing others. You might also lock layers when you have specified the exact positioning that you require and you don't want it accidentally changed while manipulating other layers. Changing the visibility of layers can also speed up editing when working on large or very detailed objects.

❑ **Notification area**: This contains hints or tricks about the objects or area you currently have selected in your document. Keep an eye on this area because it guides you with helpful information as you work within the layer. This feature is unique to Inkscape and the help messages change and update as you use the software to reflect your available options.

❑ **Pointer or cursor position**: When designing any space— either for print or web—it is often important to get the precise placement of objects. To help do this, sometimes you want to see when/where your cursor or pointer is placed on the screen. This is the area on the Inkscape main screen where you can always see the exact x (horizontal) and y (vertical) placement of your cursor within the document. The given X and Y coordinates are relative to the bottom-left corner of the document area.

❑ **Zoom**: Use the zoom tools to magnify your canvas for super close-up work or to zoom out to see the whole canvas in one shot. If you right-click the zoom field, a pop-up menu with commonly-used preset zoom levels is displayed from which you can select one to immediately adjust the canvas to. This is particularly useful with illustrations containing lots of details because you can customize your viewable magnification at any time and to whatever level you would like.

❑ **Window resize**: By default, Inkscape opens to a default window size. With this resize window option in the lower-right side of this area, you can click, hold, and drag the window to an appropriate size for your computer screen. Alternatively, you can choose to make the window full-screen by going to the main menu and choosing **View** and then **Full Screen** (press *F11* on a Windows or Linux-based system). When re-opening a .svg file, Inkscape will resize itself to the size that the window was when the file was saved. The window size information is stored in the Inkscape .svg file itself.

What just happened?

You opened the Inkscape application and familiarized yourself with the main application window.

In Inkscape, we learned that the interface itself can be a tool to help us create better designs. We reviewed:

◆ The main menu and what each option allows us to do

◆ Each of the toolbars: command, snap, tool controls, palette, and status bar and what they offer us in Inkscape

Pop quiz – using Tools

Which toolbar is the most used in Inkscape?

- a. Palette bar
- b. Snap to bar
- c. Command bar
- d. Toolbox toolbar

Understanding a new document

Now that we have learned all the menus and toolbars, let's dig into what you can do with your first open document.

Time for action – learning more about the main screen

When you open Inkscape for the first time, it opens a blank document automatically and you are ready to roll. However, you can just as easily open another new document by going to the main menu and selecting **File** | **New**.

You will be offered a number of choices of canvas sizes. Let's discuss the details of the canvas and some additional properties of the interface that you will use when opening documents.

The terms 'canvas' and 'page' are used interchangeably within the Inkscape interface. For simplicity, we'll refer to the canvas as the entire portion of the open document screen. A page is the portion of the canvas that is contained within the printable area—seen as a black-bordered box in the following screenshot:

With the main screen still open in Inkscape, let's discuss this portion of the application screen:

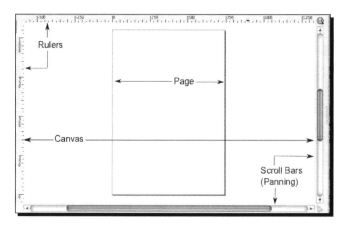

1. You can always adjust the page—or printable area—size. Go to the main menu, select **File**, and then select **Document Properties**. In the **Document Properties** window **Page** tab, look in the **Format** field. You can select any number of pre-defined sizes or change the **Custom Size** field measurements to your liking.

The pre-defined sizes are specific to print media, while those found in the main menu, **File | New** path, give common web design, logo, or web banner-sized templates.

As soon as you make changes to these properties, you can see them reflected on your screen:

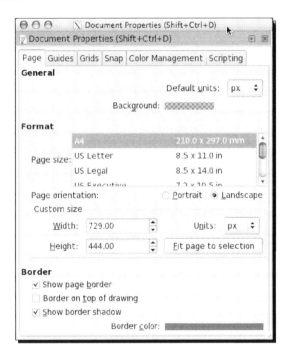

2. **Dockable dialogs** are a great feature in Inkscape 0.48. They give you more freedom in your screen layout. You can show (or hide) dialog boxes on the right-hand side of your screen:

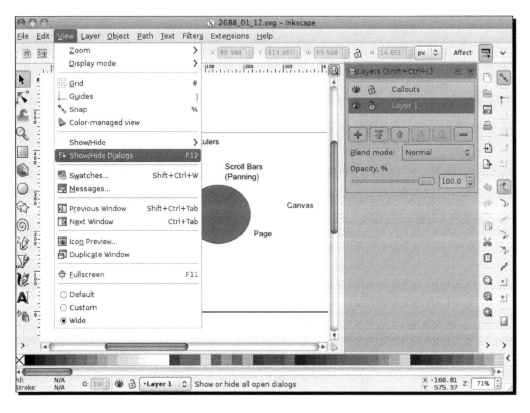

Useful dialogs that can be docked on the right-hand side of the screen are:

- **Layers**
- **Transform**
- **Path Effect**
- **SVG Font Editor**
- **Filter Editor**

The docked dialogs can be minimized, rearranged, stacked, and undocked into a separate window on your desktop. Here's how to do some of the basics:

- **Showing dialog boxes**: To show these dialog boxes, on the main menu, select **View** and select **Show/Hide Dialogs**. Then go to the **Layer**, **Object**, **Path**, or **Text** menus and choose the **Editor**, **Layer**, or **Property** options to show the correlating dialog box.

- **Displaying more than one dialog box**: If you open more than one dialog box, they will stack in the order they were opened in the dialog area of the main screen. Use the scroll bar to see those below the first viewable dialog.

- **Minimizing dialog boxes**: You can minimize a dialog so it appears as an icon. To do this, press the right arrow button, along the right-hand side of the title bar of each dialog box. This places a shortcut along the right side of the Inkscape screen. To re-open it, just click the text/icon and the dialog re-opens to the large state on the screen.

- **Floating dialog boxes**: Dialogs can also be dragged off the main window into their own window. Each dialog can have its own window or they can be grouped in floating docks.

- **Closing dialog boxes**: To close the dialog window, you can click the X on the title bar for that box. It immediately closes.

- For initial designs of any kind, these Dockable dialogs can be extremely useful. Having the **Layers** Dockable dialog visible is particularly useful, as it lets you select layers and re-order them quickly:

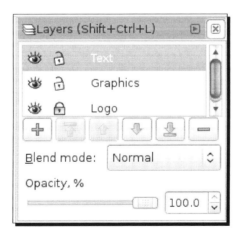

3. There are several ways to view your canvas or page in an open document. **Panning** means moving left and right, or up and down on the main screen.

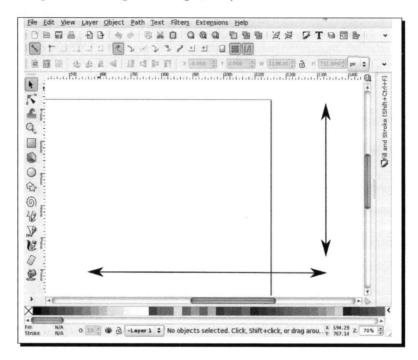

The easiest way to pan to the left or right is to use the horizontal scroll bar along the bottom of your Inkscape screen. Panning up and down can be done with the vertical scroll bar on the right-hand side of the screen. If you have a mouse with a scroll wheel you can use it to pan as well. Just scrolling with the wheel moves the canvas up and down. Pressing *Shift* on the keyboard and then using the scroll wheel moves it sideways.

As discussed in the status bar overview, you can use the zoom tool to magnify your canvas, so that you can see a lot of detail (zoomed in) or the entire canvas at a glance (zoomed out). By default, Inkscape will open documents at about 35%. You can also use the zoom tool on the toolbox [inline graphic], a mouse with a scroll wheel and the *Ctrl* key, or use your keypad (= or + zoom in and - zooms out).

For easy access to the **Zoom to fit selection**, **Zoom to fit drawing**, and **Zoom to fit page in the window** options, see options in the command bar. These options can also be set from the main menu by selecting **View | Zoom**.

What just happened?

The canvas or page in your Inkscape document can be a useful space, especially if you know how to use it best. We learned that 'canvas' and 'page' are interchangeable terms, as well as how to use scrollbars and all the intricacies of panning, zooming, and using Dockable dialogs—which will be a common item that you will return to again and again as you work on Inkscape projects.

Have a go hero – floating Dockable dialogs

Much like with the toolbars, you can move Dockable dialogs to be floating windows on your screen as well:

♦ To move any of the Dockable dialogs from their docking point on the left-hand side, click-and-drag the title bar out of the window

♦ To close the Dockable dialog, click the close button (outer-right) or click the dialog close button (on the title bar, next to icon)

♦ To re-dock the dialog, you must click-and-drag the title bar into the Dockable area

Pop quiz – new documents

What is the easiest way to open a new document within Inkscape?

a. Close down the program and re-open it

b. There isn't a way to do this via Inkscape

c. Click the new document icon on the command bar

d. From the main menu, choose **File | New**

e. Open **Document Properties** from the **File** menu.

Summary

We started this chapter by talking at a high level about Inkscape 0.48 and what you can do with it. We then jumped right into learning how to download Inkscape, detailed descriptions about how to install the software, and discussed all the main areas of the screen when opening it for the first time. We even talked a little bit about how to troubleshoot the Inkscape installation and where to find the best information about the software—no matter what your issue.

After opening our first document, we talked about changing the document properties and the value of scrolling, panning, and zooming. We even jumped into learning the basics of the software that will be key in starting our very own project. This is where we will start with *Chapter 3, How to Manage your Files*. Get ready to learn how to set up a project and get started!

3
How to Manage Files

*This chapter is all about files and managing them. Inkscape can import a
number of file formats, edit them, and save them in a number of formats.
We will discuss all of that as well as the native Inkscape SVG format, benefits
of using projects folder, and embedding versus linking image files.*

The following topics will be discussed in this chapter:

◆ Creating new files

◆ Saving Inkscape files

◆ Creating a customized default document

◆ How to structure project files

◆ Importing non-native Inkscape files

◆ Embedding and linking image files

Creating new files

As previously, stated when you first open Inkscape, a new document is opened and ready to
start. However, it uses a default size of A4. You will likely need a whole array of other sizes for
print, web design, or even custom sizes. Here's how to access all of the predefined document
dimensions Inkscape offers and details on how to adjust them manually for your needs.

Using predefined-sized document dimensions

To see all predefined document dimensions Inkscape has to offer, go the main menu and choose **File** and then **New**.

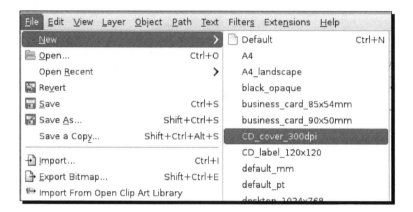

Inkscape has many predefined sizes already generated for you.

For web design, you can choose from the following:

◆ Desktops with sizes 1024 x 768, 1600 x 1200, 640 x 480, or 800 x 600

◆ Web banners with sizes 468 x 60 or 728 x 90

◆ Icon sizes ranging from 16 x 16, 32 x 32, and 48 x 48

For print, there are many sizes you can choose from:

◆ Letters: Standard US, A4

◆ Business card sizes: 84 x 54mm, 90 X 50mm

◆ CD Cover_300dpi: 343 X 340

◆ CD label: 120x120

◆ DVD covers: Regular, slim, super slim, and ultra slim

However, you can always change document dimensions to a custom size whenever you like. Just go to the main menu and select **File** and then **Document Properties**. You'll see the **Document Properties** window displayed with a number of options for customizing your canvas and *printable* page.

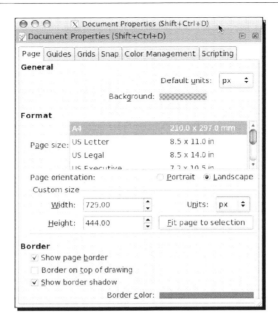

As shown in the preceding screenshot, within the **Format** field, you can choose any of the predefined values for **Page size**. Alternatively, you can use the **Custom size** field to define the size directly.

Time for action – creating a new CD cover

Imagine that you would like to use Inkscape to design and create a simple CD cover for a new music compilation you created. Here's how to get started and open a predefined template in Inkscape:

1. Open Inkscape, and from the main menu, select **File** | **New** | **CD_cover_300dpi**.

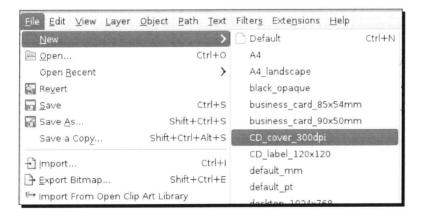

2. A new document opens to the correct dimensions.

What just happened?

Quite simply, these steps just opened up a new file in Inkscape to the exact dimensions of a CD cover.

With the autodefined templates, it takes the guesswork out of dimensions and lets you jump right into the design. We'll get back to this CD cover and design in *Chapter 4, How to build your first graphic*.

Pop quiz – how do you change the dimensions of a predefined graphic?

1. Once you open a predefined template and start working, what do you do if you need to change the dimensions?

    a. Start the design all over in a new document (from the main menu, select **File | New**).

    b. Copy and paste the design into another file.

    c. Go to the document properties (from the main menu, select **File | Document Properties**) and adjust the dimensions and fit the design.

Custom document dimensions

In the last section, we discussed creating a document that uses a predefined size already provided in Inkscape, but what if you need to create a file that is custom or not listed in the template list?

It's easy. You start with the default page size in Inkscape and then use the **Document Properties** window to adjust to the exact size you need.

Time for action – creating a new custom file size for a postcard

We're going to create a file that will be the exact size for a postcard.

1. From the Inkscape main menu, select **File | New | Default**. This opens a file with the default dimensions of A4.

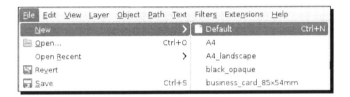

2. Now we want to customize those document dimensions. To do this, go to the main menu and choose **File | Document Properties**. You'll see the **Document Properties** window displayed with a number of options for customizing your canvas and *printable* page, as shown in the following screenshot:

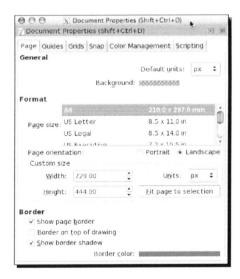

3. To change to the custom postcard size of 7 x 5 inches, we need to change the following fields in the following order: **Units** to in (Inches), **Width** to 7, and **Height** to 5. The changes on the **Document Properties** window should look similar to the following screenshot:

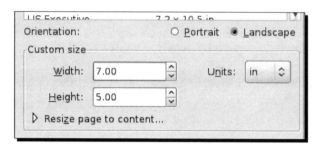

Remember to change the **Units** first; otherwise the **Width** and **Height** fields will adjust to the new unit of measure and you will have to readjust them.

Changing page orientation

Also note that you can change the **Page Orientation** from **Portrait** to **Landscape** (or vice versa) from the **Document Properties** screen. Change the field from below the **Page Size** selection box. When you do this, Inkscape automatically changes the **Width** and **Height** values already entered in the **Custom Size** section.

4. Close the **Document Properties** window/dock by clicking the **X** at the upper-right corner.

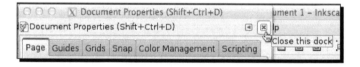

5. Your page will be resized to the new postcard custom dimensions, as shown in the following screenshot:

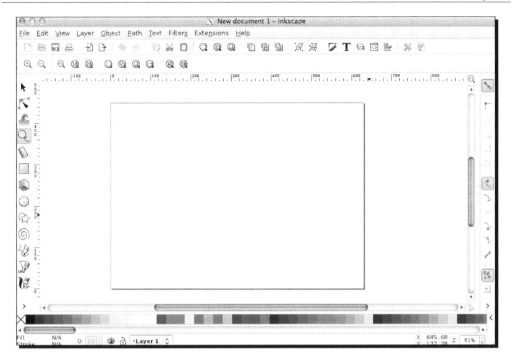

6. Keep this file open, as we will continue to manipulate it in the next section, *Have a go hero – adding a print-safe border*.

What just happened?

In a nutshell, we opened a new Inkscape file and then adjusted the document properties so that the page dimensions were set for our 7 x 5 postcard project. Now we are ready to start designing the layout of the postcard.

Have a go hero – adding a print-safe border

So now you have the page dimensions set accurately. What about setting up the file for the design? You'll need to create guides around the page edges—about one-eighth of an inch—to accommodate for printing and then cutting off the paper to size. Any and all design would need to stay within that border to be considered *print-safe*.

Here's how to set this up:

1. Open your 7 X 5 postcard file again (if it is not already open from the last exercise).
2. From the main menu, choose **File | Document Properties**.

3. In the **Document Properties** window, in the **General** section, change the **Default units** to in (inches), as shown in the following screenshot:

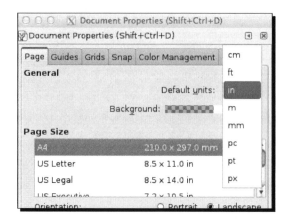

4. Now the ruler on the Inkscape screen will display units of inches.

5. Now it's time to create guides. **Guides** are lines on the screen that you will use for aligning, that is, *guiding* objects. These lines are only seen while you are working in Inkscape. To create a guide, make sure the **Select Tool** is selected, click inside the ruler area on your main screen and drag towards your page, as shown in the following screenshot. A red line represents the guide until you *let go* of the guide and place it on the page. Then the line turns blue.

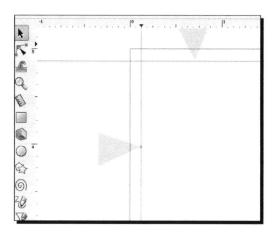

6. To make sure you position a right, left, top, and bottom guide one-eighth of an inch from each of the edges of the document, as shown in the following screenshot, you can hover over the guide line; when it turns red, double-click to bring up the dialog box to make sure the measurement is set at one-eighth of an inch. Now all of the space in the box is considered safe for design and will not be cut off during the print production of the postcards.

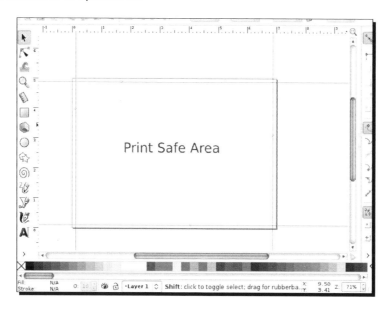

Again, we will continue to work with this file in the following exercise. Keep it open and ready for us to continue manipulating the file.

Have a go hero – adding a print bleed

What if you needed to adjust the postcard size to accommodate a bleed of the margins? A **bleed** means when an image or element on a page touches the edge of the page, often extending beyond the trim edge so there is no margin. Bleeds can extend off one or more sides of a page.

Let's begin with our print-ready postcard file from the previous section.

1. Open our 7 X 5 postcard file with the guides in place (if it is not already open from the last exercise).

2. From the main menu, choose **Extensions | Render | Printing Marks**. This will add crop and bleed marks with a specified bleed area to our canvas.

3. Create new guides (while leaving our previously created print-safe guides as is) that match the distance of the bleed marks (dotted marks).

4. Now when you design, they can bleed past the **Print Safe Area**, so they bleed to the edge of the paper when cut.

Saving Inkscape files

As you begin working on your projects, it is always good practice to save files often. Inkscape has a number of save options, in a number of formats, as well as ways to export into other common file formats.

By default, Inkscape typically saves files to your main documents folder. However, you are given an option to change this during the saving process each and every time you save a file.

Saving in Inkscape SVG

By default, Inkscape files are saved as SVG files. The native Inkscape SVG format allows editing at a later time. If file size is a concern, you can also save in the Inkscape-compressed format of SVGZ and you will have no issues editing the file and resaving it for future use.

Inkscape can save as SVG, SVGZ, PDF, PostScript/EPS/EPSi, Adobe Illustrator (*.ai), LaTex (*.tex), POVRay (*.pov), HPGL, and others. This is important because you can share files with others, which they are able to then open and manipulate.

If you work in web design, note that it is possible that you can use the SVG files directly in the HTML/XML code. However, you should work with your programming team to confirm that they can use the SVG format. (Not all browsers or platforms support this).

Saving a file in any other non-Inkscape-SVG-format could potentially make it uneditable to the extent of the original. So, always save the native Inkscape document and then export bitmaps and other graphics and/or use **File | Save Copy As** to save it in another format.

Time for action – saving an Inkscape SVG

Since you have just started using Inkscape, let's use an example file to learn about the save features of Inkscape. Open your browser and go to the following link:

```
http://www.openclipart.org/people/kuba/LGM_poster2.svg
```

Right-click on the image and select **Save As**. When prompted, save the file to a location on your computer (for example, your desktop). We will use this OpenClip Art Inkscape file for this exercise:

1. Open the example file in Inkscape.

2. Once open, from the main menu, select **File | Save**.

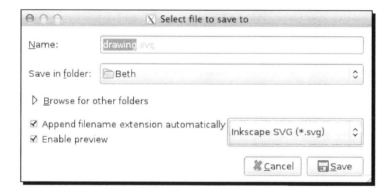

3. In the **Select file to save to** window, type a new name for your file (for example, drawing.svg).

4. Choose a folder to save the file to—including choosing **Browse for other folders** if you'd like to choose another location.

5. Again, note, by default the file will be saved as **Inkscape SVG (*.svg)**, but there are a number of other formats to choose from in this menu. However, as stated, you may lose editability of the file once saved in another non-SVG format.

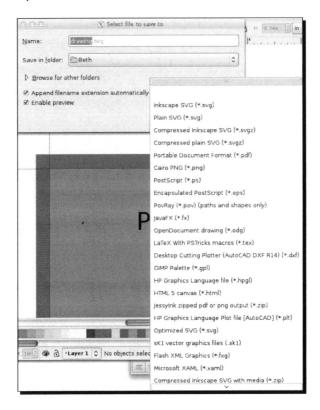

6. Click **Save**.

What just happened?

We just saved our current working file as an Inkscape (editable) SVG file—the native file format of Inkscape—to a specified location on our computer for future use.

Pop quiz – editable Inkscape file formats

1. What is the native or default Inkscape file format?

   a. VGS

   b. SVG

   c. PNG

   d. PDF

Exporting files

Inkscape's **Export Bitmap** option only allows you to export to **Portable Network Graphics** (PNG). This is an image format that uses lossless data compression.

However, there are a number of exporting options that are available.

- **Exporting a page**: Exporting the page (the bordered area) in PNG format is useful when the client wants to see a mockup of the final design for review comments or approvals—especially in web design. Mockups or wireframes allow someone to see a layout without having a need to interact with a live website.

- **Exporting a drawing**: This will export all objects in a drawing, *including* those placed outside the page (bordered area).

- **Exporting a selection**: If you have an object selected on or off the canvas, and choose this option, it will be saved as a PNG file. This is most useful for elements of a web design such as logos, wordmarks, and various other web graphics.

Time for action – exporting to PNG

Let's give this **Export** functionality a try. We'll use the postcard file we created in the previous section with a very simple design added to show how this is done.

1. With the postcard file open from the previous section, from the main menu, select **File | Export Bitmap**.

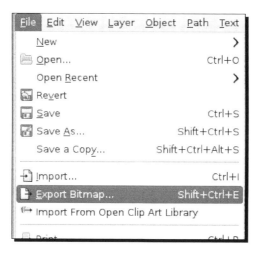

2. The **Export Window** is displayed, as shown in the following screenshot:

3. On this window, you will see a number of options along the top that detail how you might want to export the screen contents.

4. If you want to export the entire document, as shown in one bitmap image, then select **Page**.

5. If you want to export all objects in a drawing, including those placed outside the canvas/page, select **Drawing**.

6. If you want to export only a selected object (which you would see with an outline and nodes on the screen), select **Selection**. However, this option is only available if items are selected in the drawing before you start the export process.

7. Click **Browse** to change the default filename and/or the location where you want the file to be saved.

8. Click **Export**.

Your new PNG file is saved. Remember the PNG you exported from these steps won't be editable in Inkscape and the layers will not be intact, but you should be able to import it for use in another SVG file.

What just happened?

You took a project file and exported it as a PNG file type. This file type is a bitmap or rasterized graphic file type that is not editable in Inkscape, but can be imported into Inkscape to be used as part of another project.

Pop quiz – Export versus Save As

1. If you want to save a file as a PDF in Inkscape, what would you need to do?

    a. Use the **File | Export Bitmap** feature.

    b. Find another program that can open SVG files to do it for you.

    c. Use **File | Save** or **File| Save As**.

Have a go hero – saving your Inkscape file as a PDF

Since we have discussed PDF files and their importance for mockups as well as transferability between compatible software, let's learn how to save an Inkscape file as a PDF for this same purpose. PDF file sizes can typically be small and they can be opened by many programs (that are not graphics-based). In fact, you can even use PDFs for print projects or simple review files.

1. With Inkscape open and the postcard file active, from the main menu, select **File | Save**.

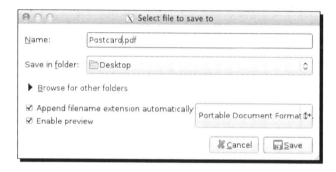

2. In the **Select file to save to** window, choose **Portable Document Format (*pdf)** as the file format.

3. In the **Name** field, type a name for your file (for example, `postcard.pdf`).

4. Choose a folder to save the file to—including choosing **Browse for other folders**, if you'd like to choose another location.

5. Click **Save**.

Creating a customized default document

When working in print design, often you might need to create a particular size document again and again. Perhaps, Inkscape does not offer this as a default size. You can then create a custom document and force Inkscape to use it as the default document size.

Time for action – creating a new default document

We're going to create a new default document with a custom size.

1. From the Inkscape main menu, select **File | New | Default**. This opens a file with the default dimensions of A4, as shown in the following screenshot:

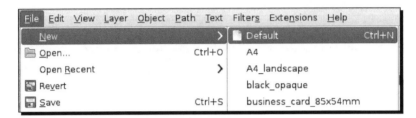

2. Now customize those document dimensions. From the main menu, choose **File | Document Properties**. You'll see the **Document Properties** window displayed, as shown in the following screenshot:

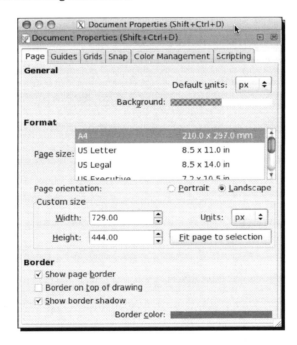

3. Change the **Units** to in (Inches), **Width** to 7, and **Height** to 5. The changes on the **Document Properties** window should look similar to the following screenshot:

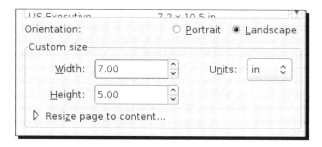

Remember to change the **Units** first; otherwise the **Width** and **Height** fields will adjust to the new unit of measurement and you will have to readjust them.

4. Close the **Document Properties** window/dock by clicking the **X** at the upper-right corner.

5. From the main menu, select **File | Save As**. Choose the following directories to save as a new default:

For Windows, save to the share directory within the Inkscape directory.
`C:\Program Files\Inkscape\share\default.svg`

For Mac and Linux users, save the file to: `/usr/share/inkscape/templates/default.svg`

6. Once saved, when you open a new Inkscape document and choose **File | New | Default**, a document with your specific dimensions will be opened.

What just happened?

We created a new default document in Inkscape and then saved it so that it will automatically open when you choose **Default** from the new file menu.

How to structure project files

The last section was about saving individual files. However, you may find yourself designing entire web pages or large projects that require more than one Inkscape file. To do this, it requires some basic organization of files within directories or folders to make finding (and using) the Inkscape files easier to use—specifically when saving entire *pages* of content as individual graphic files. The following section details how best to manage multiple file projects.

Managing multiple file projects

Simply put, if you create one directory or folder where you store all of the files for one project, you can minimize mismanagement of files. Within that directory, you will have more control over how you structure your files for revisions and drafts for work.

As stated, it starts with a project folder placed on your computer in an easy-to-access location. Whenever you create a new file in Inkscape for this project, you can save those source Inkscape files in a folder named `Source`. Then you can also create a `Deployment` folder (or another intuitive name) where you export all the files in the various formats you need to hand off to a developer for website integration or as print-ready files for a printer.

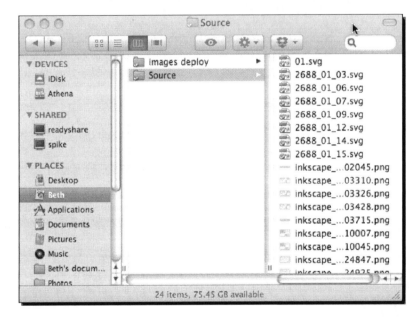

This can get a bit complicated when you decide to save all selected files on a page as individual images. Inkscape allows you to do what is called a **batch save process**. This means you save all the files with just one button press. Where it gets tricky is the save location and thus it is good practice to have directories in which to save files. Let's see how this is done.

Time for action – exporting a batch of images

We're going to look in detail at how to save an entire page or canvas of images as separate graphic files. This practice is common in web design when each image needs to be called to action in the HTML code. It can also be useful if you have developed a print design and want to save a logo, a block of text, and some graphical elements for use in another piece of the same client.

1. We will use the sample file from the previous section again for this exercise. If you have not downloaded the file, open your browser and go to the following link:

   `http://www.openclipart.org/people/kuba/LGM_poster2.svg`

   Right-click the image and save to a location on your computer.

2. Open the example file in Inkscape.

3. On the main menu, select **Edit | Select All** in **All Layers**. Now all the objects within this example file will be selected. You should see dashed borders around each object.

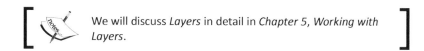 We will discuss *Layers* in detail in *Chapter 5, Working with Layers*.

4. It's time to export. From the main menu, select **File | Export Bitmap**.

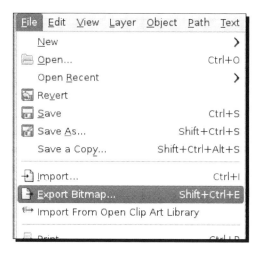

   The **Export Bitmap** window displays.

5. This time, we want to choose **Selection** from the top bar.

6. In the **Filename** field, type the directory folder that you want all object images to be saved to. If you choose to browse to a directory, you may need to select a file for the path to be accepted in this field.

7. Enable the **Batch export 8 selected objects** checkbox.

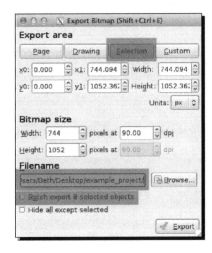

8. Click **Export**.

What just happened?

With a few simple steps in the **Export Bitmap** window, you were able to save eight objects as separate PNG files in a specified directory.

Inkscape uses object IDs when automatically assigning filenames during an export. The object IDs, by default, aren't descriptive and are often a basic description of the object with a number. However, you can rename the object ID on your canvas easily.

Renaming object IDs

In an open Inkscape document, select the object you want to rename. From the main menu, select **Object | Object Properties** (or use the *Shift + Ctrl + O* keyboard shortcut key). The **Object Properties** window is displayed. Change the **Id** field to be a descriptive filename.

Now when you export, the filename will be pulled from this **Id** field and thus be descriptive in nature for your project.

Importing non-native Inkscape files

In the previous section, we imported a previously-created Inkscape SVG file into the program. Inkscape supports a number of other graphic formats too. It can open or import SVG, SVGZ (gzipped SVG), PDF, and AI (Adobe Illustrator) formats. In particular, it can import bitmap-based graphic formats such as JPEG, PNG, and GIF, but it can only export PNG bitmaps.

With the help of extensions and plugins, Inkscape can also open a number of other vector formats. The following are some examples:

♦ For importing PostScript or EPS, install Ghostscript (http://pages.cs.wisc. edu/~ghost/)

♦ For formats of Dia, XFig, or Sketch, you need to have those programs installed on your computer

♦ For CorelDraw, CGM, and SK1 files, install Uniconverter (http://sk1project. org/). For Windows users, Uniconvertor is pre-installed with Inkscape and no additional installation is needed.

See this version of the Inkscape manual for the fully-supported formats and the caveats of importing each: http://tavmjong.free.fr/INKSCAPE/MANUAL/html/File-Import. html.

Remember, if you import and open a non-native Inkscape file, you may not be able edit all of the elements. Inkscape imports non-native files as flattened graphic files, so you can't edit anything within the graphic, but you can manipulate or use the flattened image within Inkscape.

 The recommended format for transferring non-native Inkscape files is to use the original source program and files to create a PDF. Then open the PDF in Inkscape. PDF files, when imported into Inkscape, allow for editability to remain with vector-based objects.

Time for action – importing a PDF into Inkscape

Let's import a non-native Inkscape SVG file into Inkscape—as you may need to do this for client logos, photographs, and any number of other real-world examples. Open a browser and go to this link: `http://db.tt/xR0ZlBRL`

A PDF will be downloaded and saved to your computer. It will be our sample file to work with during this exercise.

1. Open a document in Inkscape. This can be any in-progress file that we have used previously in this chapter, or a new document.

2. From the main menu, select **File | Import**.

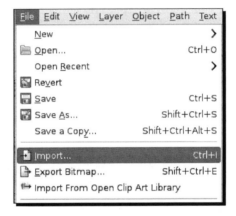

The **Select file to import** window displays, as shown in the following screenshot:

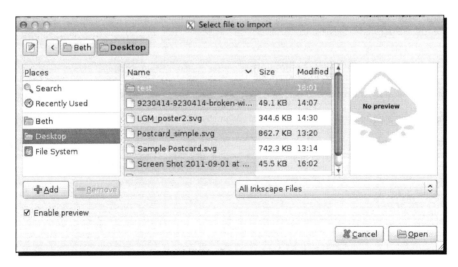

3. Locate and select the sample PDF file you just downloaded and select **Open**.

4. When the **PDF Import Settings** screen displays, adjust settings as needed and click **OK**.

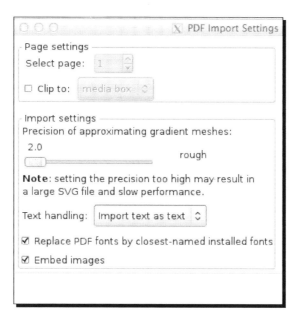

5. Within **Page settings**, you can choose whether you want all pages of the PDF to be imported or just a specific page number. The **Clip to** field has various options (**media box**, **crop box**, **trim box**, **bleed box**, **art box**, and so on), allowing you to determine how the file is imported into your current canvas.

6. Within **Import settings**, you can set the **Precision of Gradient Meshes**. Any gradients seen on your objects are converted to tiny boxes. The higher the precision, the more boxes will be used to illustrate the gradient (also, the larger the file size, the slower the load time in Inkscape).

7. Depending on the source application that created the PDF, you can adjust **Text handling**. If you choose **Import text as text**, all the text objects will be brought in as such in Inkscape and then become editable.

8. The checkboxes on the screen allow for you to replace fonts to the closest match (checked) and to embed images (checked).

9. In a few moments, the PDF file you selected will display within the page of your Inkscape project.

Note that this imported PDF *is* fully editable if the objects are vector-based. Rasterized images are more limited to the following:

- ◆ Moving the object: Click to select it and move it to where you want it to be on the canvas.
- ◆ Making the image smaller: Double-click the object to select and click-and-drag an arrowed corner to shrink it.

Any detailed edits such as changing color or moving lines within the PDF are not permissible. However, the object is fully usable within the Inkscape file for design purposes. Photographs and similar rasterized images can all be used in this fashion.

Edit text blocks

To edit an imported block of text like a typewriter, select the text block and **Remove Manual Kerns** from the **Text Menu**.

What just happened?

We imported a sample PDF file into Inkscape to demonstrate the flexibility of this file format. If objects are vector-based, they maintain editability. If rasterized images are included, then they have more limited editing capabilities.

Pop quiz – file format portability

1. What is the ideal format for transferring non-native Inkscape files to Inkscape?

    a. SVG

    b. JPG

    c. GIF

    d. PDF

Embedding and linking image files

When you import files into Inkscape, you are prompted about linking or embedding them. **Linking** a file means that the file is essentially displayed within your Inkscape document and there are associated properties (location, size, and so on) to that linked object. The original file must remain in the exact location on your computer or you will not be able to view it in the Inkscape file and any changes you make to the original file will be seen in the Inkscape file.

Embedding a file means that the file itself is brought into the Inkscape document and it resides there. All changes made to that file within your project stay within your project and the original source file can be moved to any location on your computer.

The advantage to embedding images is that they are not tied to the original source. You can move the source file or the Inkscape file anywhere on your computer or even send a co-worker the Inkscape file and there is no need to worry about the linked file. However, this also means your file sizes will be larger.

There are some limitations to embedding images into the Inkscape SVG files. They are as follows:

♦ For SVG files used directly on the web, increasing the file size increases bandwidth usage on the server or host.

♦ Embedded images can't be shared across documents. For example, if you have one PNG image as a background file, you can't share it across SVG files.

♦ Sharing copyrighted fonts or images in a document could be illegal (depending on how extensive the rights you have purchased to use these items are to begin with). This is particularly important when working on commercial or widely-used projects.

♦ If there is extensive text editing within the SVG files themselves, this can be complicated and time-intensive.

Linking keeps file sizes small, but you must remember to send all additional files along with your Inkscape SVG files when you go to production or create print-ready PDFs; otherwise all linked objects will not display.

Embedding files in Inkscape

The best examples for embedding files in Inkscape are when you want one all-inclusive file that can be sent or posted individually without worrying about additional source files or directory structures. Another example could be when you know that you will change the location of the linked or Inkscape file frequently, as you work with different versions.

Time for action – embedding a logo into your design

Let's learn how to embed a logo file into a design. We'll start by downloading a sample logo. Open a browser and go to this Open Clipart sample logo at the following URL:

```
http://www.openclipart.org/image/800px/svg_to_png/vetlogo.png
```

Right-click on the logo and save it to your computer.

1.   Open a document in Inkscape.

2.   From the main menu, select **File | Import**. Alternatively, you can drag-and-drop a file from your desktop onto an open Inkscape file.

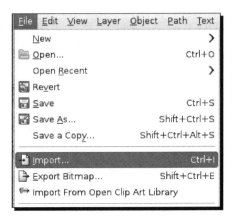

The **Select file to import** window displays.

3.   Locate and select the `Sample` logo file you just downloaded and select **Open**.

4.   When the input screen displays, select **Embed**.

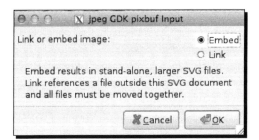

5.   Click **OK**.

6.   In a few moments, the logo you selected displays and is embedded within the page of your Inkscape project.

What just happened?

In the preceding steps, you embedded a logo image into your current Inkscape document.

Linking external files in Inkscape

Linking certain files can be useful—particularly if the source file you want to link to is a large, high-resolution photograph.

Time for action – linking a photograph into a brochure design

Now let's try to link external files into an Inkscape project. For this example, we will just use the same logo as the previous example. If you did not download it yet, open a browser and go to the following Open Clipart sample logo:

```
http://www.openclipart.org/image/800px/svg_to_png/vetlogo.png
```

Right-click on the logo and save it to your computer.

1. Open a document in Inkscape.

2. From the main menu, select **File | Import**.

   The **Select file to import** window is displayed.

3. Locate and select the Sample logo file you just downloaded and select **Open**.

4. When the input screen displays, this time select **Link**.

5. Click **OK**.

6. In a few moments, the logo you selected displays and is embedded within the page of your Inkscape project.

 You moved your source file and now need to change the link path to your file?

Right-click on your linked object in your Inkscape file and select **Image Properties**. Change the **URL** field to match the new path to the file.

What just happened?

You linked an image file into your current open Inkscape project and learned a special tip for fixing a broken image link in any of your old files.

Pop quiz – linking versus embedding images

1. Why would you want to link an external file instead of an embedded one?

    a. A large image size

    b. The image will be constantly changing and you want the changes to be reflected instantly in your Inkscape file

    c. Project file structure will remain the same and there are a limited number of images

    d. All of the above

Have a go hero – changing your mind, embedding files after the fact

What if you initially linked all files and then decide that you would rather embed them all? The following are the steps to take to make this happen:

1. Open an Inkscape document.

2. From the main menu, select **Extensions**, then **Images**, and **Embed Images....**

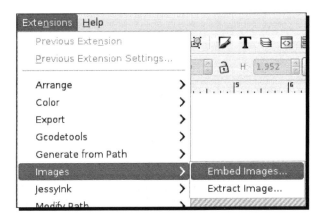

3. Do not check the **Embed only selected images** box.

If you want to embed only certain images in the document, then you must select those images first. You should then go to the main menu, select **Extensions** | **Images** | **Embed Images...**, and check the **Embed only selected images** box.

4. Click **Apply**.

Summary

We spent the majority of this chapter discussing how to create new files in Inkscape. You learned how to use predefined page/canvas sizes in Inkscape, how to customize the file size, and even how to create print bleeds and the setup for print-safe space on your documents.

Then we jumped into saving Inkscape files—paying close attention to discuss the advantages of keeping a source version of all documents in Inkscape's native file format of SVG, so you can continue to edit your files. Along with that topic, we jumped into managing multiple file projects and best practices, the details regarding which formats in which Inkscape can save, as well as importing file types. Finally, we talked about embedding and linking files and images in your Inkscape files. We detailed the advantages and disadvantages of each approach as well as how to work with both in your files for the best experience.

All of this is leading up to the next chapter, which deals with starting your very first Inkscape project. We've done a lot of preparation; now it is time to start designing!

4

Creating your First Graphics

We're now ready to create some graphics. We'll start with some basic shapes and then move on to freehand objects, using grids and guidelines to help to create better graphics better create graphics.

The following are the specifics about what we will learn:

- ◆ Paths and Shapes
- ◆ Creating your first vector graphic
- ◆ Ellipses and Arcs
- ◆ Complex Shapes
- ◆ Freehand Objects
- ◆ Using Grids and Guidelines

Paths

Vector graphics are made up of what are called geometrical primitives such as points, lines, curves, and shapes. These primitives then have a start and end point, curves, angles, and points that are calculated with a mathematical equation. These paths are not limited to being straight—they can be of any shape, size, and even encompass any number of curves. When you combine them, they create drawings, diagrams, and can even help create certain fonts.

Inkscape uses both paths and a series of pre-determined shapes when creating graphics. Paths have no predefined lengths or widths. They are arbitrary in nature and come in three basic types:

- ◆ Open paths (have two ends)
- ◆ Closed paths (have no ends, like a circle)
- ◆ Compound paths (use a combination of two or more open and/or closed paths)

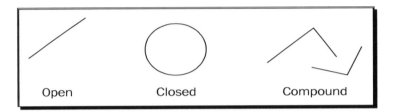

| Open | Closed | Compound |

In Inkscape, there are a few ways we can make paths such as with the Pencil (Freehand), Bezier (Pen) , and Calligraphy tools—all of which are found in the toolbox located at the left side of your screen.

You can also convert a regular shape or text object into a path.

In general, we use paths to build unique objects that aren't part of the SVG standard shapes in Inkscape. Since we can combine paths and make them closed objects—they again can be resized, manipulated, and then exported in a number of formats.

Creating your first vector graphic

In this section, we will show you how to create some basic vector graphics with shapes and paths in Inkscape (which thankfully doesn't require you to do any mathematical equations when using it) and export them in a couple of different formats.

Here are the standard shapes that are part of the SVG standard:

◆   Rectangles, squares, and 3D boxes

◆   Circles, ellipses, and arcs

◆   Stars and polygons

◆   Spirals

Creating a polygon

Let's break down creating our first graphic—a star—into many smaller substeps just to get started. We will do the following:

◆   Open a new document

◆   Create the polygon object

◆   Change the object properties

◆   Save our graphic

Let's get started!

Time for action – opening a new document

When you first open Inkscape, a new document is opened and you are ready to start. However, it uses a default canvas size of A4 and you may need to change the orientation and size for the graphic you are creating, as follows:

1.   Open Inkscape.

2.   If you need to create a new document, go to **File | New**. A menu appears with the predefined sizes Inkscape has for you.

3. If you want to manually change your document properties, just go to the main menu and select **File | Document Properties**. You will see the **Document Properties** window displayed with a number of options for customizing your canvas size.

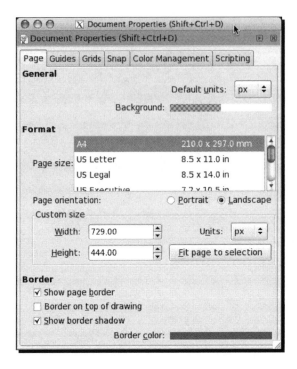

4. If you want to change the default background color (default in Inkscape is a transparent background), you change it in the **General**, **Background** section. Click the color swatch to change it.

5. If you want to adjust any Border settings, check the appropriate checkboxes. The options include:

- ❑ Showing a page border
- ❑ Showing the border on top of any objects on the canvas
- ❑ Showing a border shadow

6. When complete, close the **Document Properties** window by clicking the X in the upper-left corner and your changes will be reflected in the main window.

What just happened?

We opened Inkscape and adjusted the canvas size for your graphic. We also discussed additional document properties that can be changed such as background color, page border options, and border shadows.

Pop quiz – displaying borders

1. Why might it be important to have borders show on top of your drawing objects?

    a. If you are using page borders as cropping/print guidelines, you know where the final paper will be cut

    b. It isn't important at all

    c. Gives great artistic flare to the graphic

Time for action – creating a star

Now, we will create a shape that is a part of the SVG standard that is inherent in Inkscape. These standard shapes include rectangles/squares, circles/ellipses/arcs, stars, polygons, and spirals. We will create a star. Here's what you need to do:

1. Select (click) the shape tool icon (A) and the polygon icon (B) in the toolbox, as highlighted in the following screenshot.

2. Then draw the shape on the canvas by clicking, holding, and then dragging the shape to the size you want on the canvas:

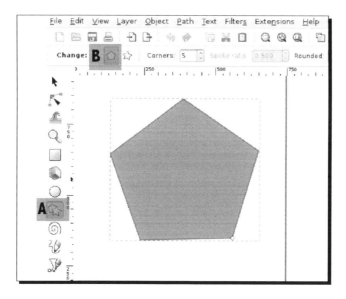

3. To switch between creating stars and polygons, select the star/polygon icon in the toolbox on the left-hand side of your screen, and then select either the polygon or the star icon in the Tool controls (just above the canvas).

4. You can also change the number of corners this polygon has by changing the number in the **Corners** field in the Tool controls.

If you had wanted to draw a circle, square, or cube—you would have selected those icons on the toolbox.

It is possible that your star doesn't match the one shown in the preceding screenshot. Maybe your color or border is different. That is because, when you opened Inkscape, your color palette settings were set to the last used style. The *Have a go Hero – changing the unit of measure*, section explains how to change those settings—**Fill** and **Stroke**—so your star can look similar to the example.

What just happened?

You created a star object on your blank canvas.

Pop quiz – switching shapes

1. What if you decided instead of a star, you would like to draw a cube. In which screen toolbar would you look for the correct tool?

    a.   Palette bar

    b.   Tool controls

    c.   Toolbox

    d.   Object dialog

Have a go hero – changing shape options

Shapes have a number of attributes or options. By default those attributes will be the last-used style (for example, color). In Inkscape, the user interface gives you easy-to-use tools to change options such as fill color, stroke color, size, and placement of the shape.

1. Change the fill color of the shape by selecting a color in the color palette.

2. Change the stroke or border color by pressing and holding the *Shift* key and then selecting that color from the color palette.

3. Change the position of the shape on the canvas by choosing the Select tool in the toolbox, clicking and holding the shape, and moving it to where you need it to be.

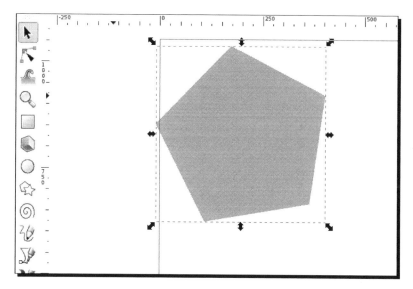

4. Change the size of the shape by also choosing the Select tool from the toolbox, clicking and holding the edge of the shape at the handles (small black square or circles at the edges), and dragging it outwards to make it larger or inwards to shrink until the shape is of the desired size.

    The shape is still fully editable and the number of tips in the star is adjusted through the tool controls bar. You can also switch between polygon and stars.

Time for action – saving your graphic

After you have created an initial version of your graphic, it is best practice to save your file so that you don't lose any work. This is a simple example graphic, so you may not want to save the file, but for any future work, this step is critical.

1. With your latest project open, from the main menu select **File | Save**. Inkscape will, by default, give options to save projects in its default format, SVG. Choose a file location and click **Save**.

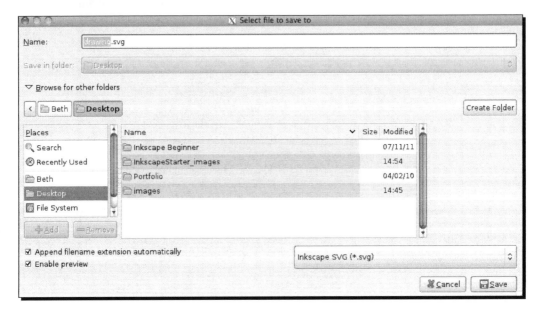

2. However, you might also want to export in a bitmap graphic format such as PNG. To do this, choose **File | Export Bitmap**.

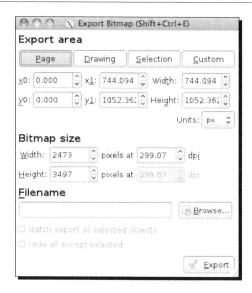

3. In the **Export Bitmap** window, you can choose to save the **Page** (all objects within the page/black border, the **Drawing** (all objects), the **Selection** (only the object you have selected), or customize it.

4. Choose the **Export** area, the graphic size you want (will select predefined size by default), and click **Browse** to choose the same location.

5. Verify the filename in the textbox and click **Export**.

6. To save in another format besides PNG, go to **File | Save As** and choose the file format of your choice. Inkscape allows you to save in a number of formats such as PDF, EPS, ODG, WMF, among others. However, remember that if you want to save the file in a format that will allow you to edit in the future, you need to save it in Inkscape SVG.

What just happened?

You saved your graphics file as a native Inkscape SVG file so you can edit it later, and then exported it into another format (as needed).

Pop quiz – image formats

1. What is the only bitmap format that Inkscape can export to?

    a. JPG

    b. GIF

    c. BMP

    d. PNG

Creating ellipses and arcs

Now, we're going to get a bit fancier and create ellipses and arcs. Ellipses are of oval shape. To start, we will create an ellipse and explain how to make perfect circles and then details about creating an arc.

Time for action – creating the Ellipse

Let's start by creating an ellipse.

1. With a new document open in Inkscape, select the circle tool or ellipse tool.

2. On the canvas, press the *Ctrl* key, click, hold, and drag the shape to the size you want on the canvas.

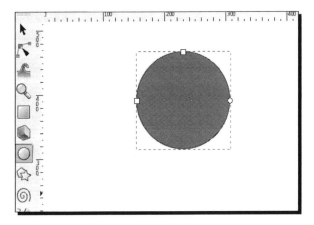

What just happened?

You created a circle on your canvas.

1. How can you make a perfect circle in Inkscape?

    a. Freehand it with the freehand tool.

    b. Use a star and clipping masks.

    c. Use the circle tool in the toolbox and press the *Ctrl* key while resizing it.

    d. None of the above.

Time for action – making an arc

Now, we will take our circle and convert it into an arc.

1. Make sure that the **Circle/Ellipse** tool is still selected and you can see the handles on the shape on the canvas.

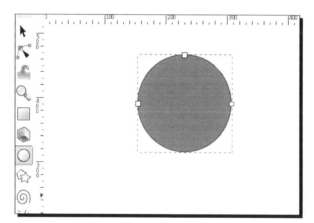

Notice, there are three handles which are top (square), left (square), and right (circle). To control the horizontal and vertical dimensions, you use the top (horizontal) and left (vertical) handles.

Dragging the right circle handle of a whole ellipse creates an arc or segment.

To switch between an arc or pie segment, drag the handle inside or outside of the ellipse. Let's give it a try.

2. Drag an arc handle (the circle one) to set one end of the arc. Once you *pull* or drag one of the arc handles, you will see that there are actually two overlapping arc handles for you to manipulate. (as shown in the following screenshot, this is now a closed path).

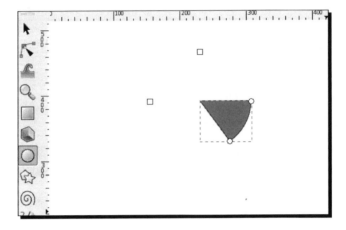

Drag the second arc handle (in the original position) to the other end of the arc, The arc will be closed and a pie shape will be created (an open path).

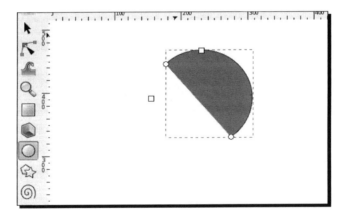

3. Hold the *Ctrl* key while dragging an arc handle to force the angle of the arc to begin or end at a multiple of the rotation snap angle (15 degrees by default). To precisely place objects on the canvas, an object is made to snap to a target that is an object, guide, grid, or in this case an angle. Drag one of the arc handles outside the curve of the original ellipse (outside the dashed box); the arc handle icon turns blue and a wedge is created at the center of the shape (again, a closed path).

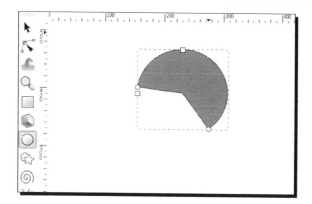

4. If the arc handle is dragged with the cursor inside the curve, the segment defining the arc starts and stops at the two arc handles, as shown in the following screenshot (now an open path).

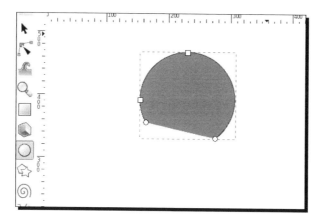

5. Once the arc is created and selected on the canvas, you can use the **Tool controls** bar to set specific locations (in degrees) for the start and stop arc handles.

Also, note in the toolbar, the buttons that can quickly change an ellipse into a closed path or an open path. The one selected in the preceding screenshot is an open path; whereas the one to the left is a closed path.

The full circle button resets the ellipse to whole. When creating ellipses, the *next* one you create will use the *last used style* (for example, after this exercise it would be an arc). The Reset ellipse button will then become handy to start anew.

What just happened?

You took a simple circle and created a number of arcs—essentially learning the skills that you need to manipulate arcs in Inkscape.

Complex Shapes

As a designer you will often want to create logos or shapes that are outside the standard ones provided in the software. Since Inkscape is vector-based, you can combine simple shapes, masking, hiding, and layering them to create more complex shapes. Let's perform a simple example to see how this can be done.

Time for action – combining shapes

One of the simplest ways to create complex shapes in Inkscape is to combine other shapes into one or merge the shapes. Let's learn how we can do this by creating an arrow with a polygon and rectangle shape.

1. Open a new document (any size will do, since we are just practicing).

2. Select the **Polygon** tool from the toolbox.

3. Create a polygon shape.

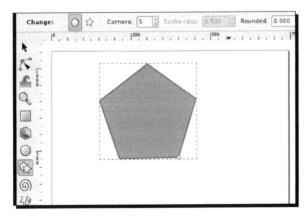

4. From the Tool controls, change **Corners** to **3**, as shown in the following screenshot:

The octagon polygon shape changes to a triangle.

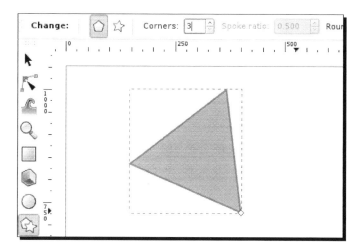

5. From the toolbox, choose the **Select** tool and click the triangle object twice. The handles turn to curved arrows so you can rotate the triangle as shown in the following screenshot:

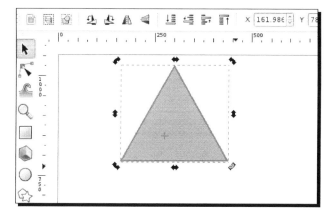

Rotating an object

While drawing the polygon on the canvas, you can swivel it up, down, left, and right. Use the *Ctrl* key while performing the following actions and it will make rotations snap in 15 degree increments.

It is okay if you don't do this while drawing it initially, you can always choose the **Select** tool from the toolbox, and click the polygon until the handles turn to arrows with curves (this might require you to click the polygon object a couple of times). When you see the curved arrow handles, click-and-drag on a corner node to rotate the object until it is positioned correctly.

6. From the toolbox, select the rectangle tool and draw a rectangle just below the triangle on the canvas.

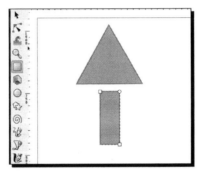

7. Now, choose the **Select** tool from the toolbox, and drag the rectangle so it creates the stem of the arrow as follows:

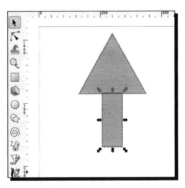

8. To readjust the size of the rectangle, make sure the **Select** tool is active, and click the rectangle. The resize handles appear. Click the handle on a side that needs to be adjusted and drag it to resize.

9. With the rectangle still selected, press and hold the *Shift* key, and click the triangle so that all objects are selected.

10. From the main menu select **Path | Union**:

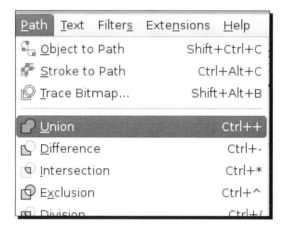

This merges the two shapes into one... and voila, it's an arrow!

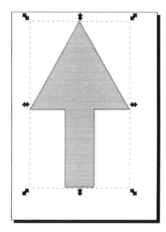

What just happened?

You created a polygon, changed the number of corners, created a rectangle and combined them—or joined them—into a union to create an arrow object. Technically, the shapes were transformed into a path. The shape tools no longer work on this object and it is its own object in Inkscape that can be resized and manipulated like any other object.

Pop quiz – joining objects

1. How do you join more than one shape in Inkscape?

   a. Select all the objects you want to join together and then on the main menu select **Path | Union.**

   b. You can't.

   c. You have to draw an object freehand.

Freehand objects (Paths)

You can also use the **Bezier (Pen)** or **Freehand Tool** to create objects in a bit more freehand form. This tool allows you to create straight lines and curves and connect them to create a freehand object.

Time for action – creating a freehand object

Here's an example of how to create a lightning bolt.

1. From a new document, choose the **Bezier** tool from the **Tool Box**.

2. Click somewhere on the canvas to start drawing a straight line, click to establish a node, click again to change direction of the straight line to create an angle in our lightning bolt, as shown in the following screenshots:

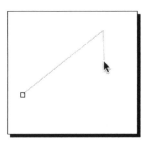

3. Continue to create the lightning bolt object by creating the shape segment by segment.

Don't worry if you stop a line and realize you need to extend its length, just click and move a straight line to add on to the original to make it as long as you need. Click again when you are ready to change direction. If you made a mistake, press the *Backspace* or *Delete* key and it removes the last line segment.

4. To *close* the lightning bolt, just create a line segment and join it to the starting point with a final click. The start node will *glow* red in color when the mouse is hovered over it for easy identification. This is helpful to make sure that the close of the object is done correctly. You will see that all the lines are combined into one continuous closed path—a lightning bolt.

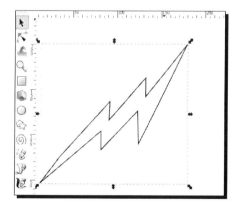

When you select the lightning bolt, the entire object is selected. You can resize it, fill it with a color (select it and choose a color from the color palette), and move it to another location on the canvas. It has become a unique object for you to work with.

The **Bezier** tool also allows you to create controlled curves to create even more complex and unique objects. Try creating objects on your own and experimenting. These complex objects can be used for icons, banners, and for unique logo designs.

What just happened?

You used the **Bezier** tool and created, in multiple small steps, a lightning bolt.

Pop quiz – deleting

1. What are the important keys to remember if you want to delete the last line you drew with the Bezier Tool?

   a. *D* key

   b. *Shift* key

   c. *Enter* key

   d. *Backspace* or *Delete* key

Using grids and guidelines

When designing, we often need to align objects for a clean look. To do this, grids can be used to help in alignment. We will start this section by learning how to turn the canvas grid on, set up snap to alignment, and then how to set up guidelines.

Time for action – viewing the Grid

We will start with the easiest task, turning the Grid on (or making it viewable).

1. With your new document still open on your computer, on the Inkscape main menu select **View | Grid**:

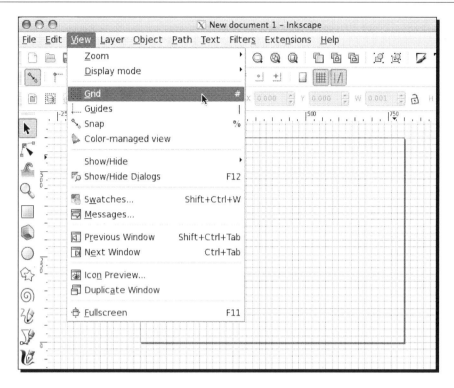

What just happened?

You'll see that a blue grid will appear across the entire canvas area. We will use these grids to create basic areas of our layout and then create guides to begin creating our actual layout elements.

Have a go hero – changing the unit of measure

By default, Inkscape keeps all dimensions—even the unit of measure—in pixels. Do you want your grid to be in inches? There is an easy way to do this.

1. Go to the main menu, choose **File | Document Properties**. You'll see the **Document Properties** window displayed.

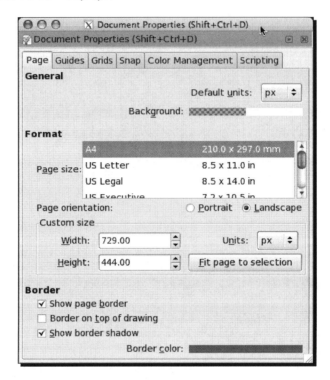

2. Change the **Units** field to **in** (Inches). This will change the grid, the canvas dimensions, and all units of measure to inches in this document.

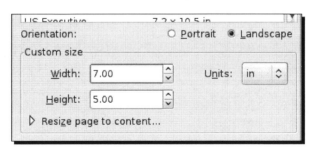

Pop quiz – viewable grid

1. What is the shortcut key for making Grids viewable in Inkscape?

    a. The *G* key

    b. *F1*

    c. *#*

    d. *Enter*

Time for action – making guides

Now it's time to create guides. Guides are lines on the screen that you will use for aligning, that is, *guiding* objects. These lines are only visible while you are working in Inkscape and we can set objects to *snap to* them when we are designing. Both of these simple tools (guides and the Snap to feature) will give you automatic alignment for the basic areas of your web page layout—which in turn will help make the design process much easier.

1. To create a guide in any open document, drag from the left or top ruler toward your page as in the following screenshot. A red line represents the guide until you *let go* of the guide and place it on the page. Then the line turns blue.

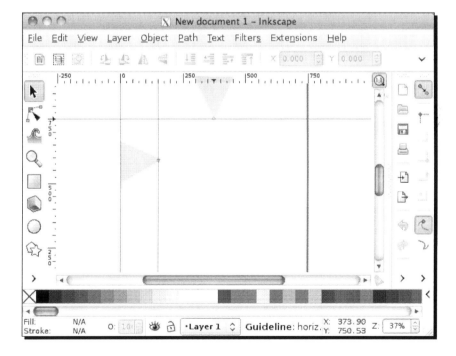

You can move the guides after placing them on the page by using the Select tool and clicking-and-dragging the circle node on the guide. Also, double-clicking directly on a guide will bring up a dialog box which lets you change the guide positions and angle very accurately.

What just happened?

You created two guidelines on your current canvas: one from the right ruler and one from the top.

One note here, if you want to make multiple guidelines, even on the right side of the canvas, it is easy. Just *drag* from the left ruler onto the canvas over other guidelines and all rulers currently placed on the page and *drop* it where you need it on the page. There is no maximum number of guidelines that you can create.

Summary

We created our very first graphics from polygons, ellipses, circles, arcs, and even an arrow by combining shapes. To do all of this, we used the basic shapes available to us through Inkscape but also worked with the Bezier Tool to create freehand shapes (such as the lightning bolt).

We also took some time to turn on grids and to learn how to create guides for better aligning and designing. Next up, we shall be learning all we can about layers.

5
How to Work with Layers

*If you have used any other graphics program, you are likely to be familiar with layers. **Layers** are like stacks of transparent paper with drawings on them. Each layer stacks, and thus objects on each of the layers also stack on top of one another. Of course when using layers in Inkscape, you can manipulate all of the objects in one layer the same way.*

This chapter will cover:

- ◆ Defining layers and how to create them
- ◆ Using layers in an example drawing
- ◆ Locking layers
- ◆ Hiding layers
- ◆ Dockable Layer dialog
- ◆ Duplicating layers
- ◆ Arranging layers
- ◆ Renaming layers
- ◆ Deleting layers
- ◆ Blend mode

Defining layers and how to create them

Within Inkscape when you create documents you can have layers of objects. This gives great flexibility when creating any Inkscape project. You can place groups of objects on a layer based on function or placement on the design. Then you can separate the objects by layer, and stack or reorder, or hide layers. A setting can be adjusted on each layer, so you can save drafts or different versions of mockups and keep all of this in one file.

The layer you are currently using is called the **drawing layer**. It is selected in the **Layer** dialog and shown in a darker color.

Also note, you can view Inkscape layers in the **Layer** dialog or in a drop-down menu in the status bar:

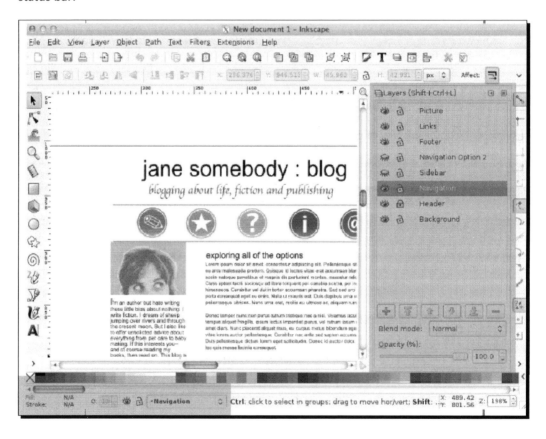

Time for action – creating a layer

Let's start by creating a customized layer. We'll call it **Basic Layout**.

1. First, let's make the **Layers** dockable dialog viewable. From the main menu, select **Layer** and then select **Layers**. The **Layers** dialog is displayed on the right-hand side of your screen as follows:

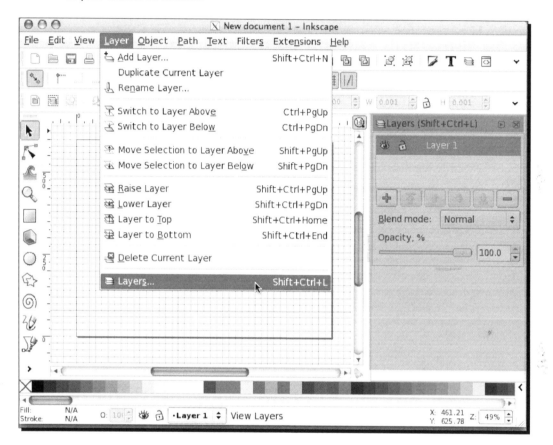

 You can also press *Shift + Ctrl + L* on your keyboard or click the **Layers** icon in the command bar (as shown in the following screenshot) to display the **Layers** dialog.

2. In the **Layers** dialog, press the + button to create a new layer or use the *Shift + Ctrl + N* shortcut keys. The default layer is called **Layer 1**. However, you can rename it, move it up and down in the stack, and it is treated no different than any other layer you create in your projects.

3. In the **Layer name** field, type the name: **Basic Layout** and click **Add**:

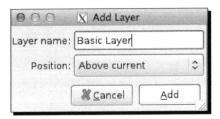

You will notice the new layer is added above the existing one in the Layers dialog as follows:

What just happened?

You created a new layer in an open document in Inkscape called **Basic Layout**. You will need to repeat the steps mentioned earlier every time you want to create a new layer.

Pop quiz – Layers dialog

1. How do you close the **Layers** dialog?

    a. From the main menu, select **Layer** and then select **Layers**.

    b. Press the X on the upper-right side of the **Layers** dialog window.

   c.   Once it is open, you cannot close the **Layers** dialog window.

   d.   Close Inkscape all together and re-open it.

Using Layers in an example drawing

Let's create the basic links for a blog. Some common parts of many blog sites are the blog header or banner, a sidebar with recent posts (or archives), an about section, recent posts, blog roll and/or a Links section, and a main content section that will contain all of the blog posts. Of course, you can get as fancy as you like here, or as simple, but let's design a site based on these simple sections so we can demonstrate how to use layers to create a design layout mockup.

Time for action – using Layers in web design

To start, we will create the very start of a website, or more specifically a blog, and create three layers in the design:

1.   Open Inkscape, and create a new document. From the file menu, select **File | New | Desktop_800x600**.

2.   From the main menu, choose **File | Document Properties**.

3.   Click on **Background**. The **Background color** dialog will be displayed.

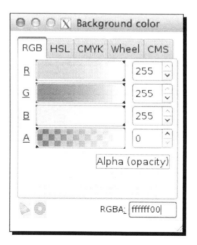

4.   Change RGBA from **ffffff00** to **ffffffff**. This will change the background color of this screen mockup to white.

5. In the **Layer** dialog, click the + sign to create a new layer (or use *Shift + Ctrl + N*) and call it **Header**.

6. Click the **Create and Edit Objects** tool and enter the header title for the blog.

You could try creating something similar to the following screenshot:

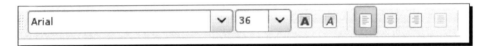

7. Highlight the text with the **Create and Edit Objects** tool and use the control bar located above the canvas area and adjust the font type and size. In the previous example, the font type is **Arial** and it is **36** points in size, as shown in the following screemshot:

8. Then, still using the **Create and Edit** tool, type the subtitle as shown in the example. Remember to use the control bar to adjust the font type and size. In the same (previous) example, the font for the subtitle is **Apple Chancery** with an **18** point font.

9. Next, we want to center both of these titles on the vertical axis of this document. Use the Select tool, press the *Shift* key on the keyboard, and click both titles (this will allow you to select both objects).

10. Click the **Align and Distribute Objects** icon on the command bar to display the **Align and Distribute** dialog, as shown in the following screenshot:

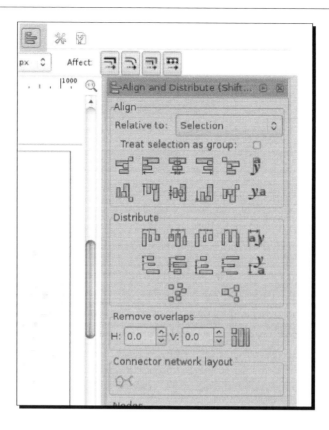

11. Click the **Center on Vertical Axis** icon. This will center both title objects on the page:

12. Now we will add a new layer yet again. Create the new layer by using the **Layer** dialog, + sign, or the *Shift + Ctrl + N* shortcut keys. Let's call the layer **Navigation**.

13. For the navigational elements, we will import some ready-made icons. First download the icons to your hard drive from http://dl.dropbox. com/u/565455/iconpack.zip.

14. Unzip these icons to your hard drive, preferably on your desktop. From the desktop then drag-and-drop your icon files onto the Inkscape canvas. Repeat this until you have all five icons on the canvas. See the following sample screenshot:

15. To make sure you have everything evenly spaced, we need to align them. Click the **Align and Distribute Objects** icon on the command bar to display the **Align and Distribute** dialog if it is still not displayed.

16. Choose the **Select** tool, press the *Shift* key and click on all icons.

17. In the **Align and Distribute** dialog, click the **Distribute Centers Equidistantly Horizontally** button.

This will make sure all of the icons are spaced equally apart from one another to make a clean design.

What just happened?

In the small example mentioned earlier, you created three layers: **Background**, **Header**, and **Navigation**, each with the object associated with them. If you continue this process, you can build something similar to what is given in the following screenshot that has additional layers side content, body content, and footer, for example. To see this project in its complete form, you can download it from `http://dl.dropbox.com/u/565455/ exampleprojectlayout.svg`.

jane somebody : blog

blogging about life, fiction and publishing

I'm an author but hate writing these little bios about nothing. I write fiction. I dream of sheep jumping over rivers and through the cresent moon. But I also like to offer unsolicited advice about everything from pet care to baby making. If this interests you-- and of course reading my books, then read on. This blog is for you.

favorite rants

● writing not for the faint of hear (or in other words, there is no magic potion to publishing)

● dreaming of sheep and rivers

● my existence is futile

● a non-existent attempt at life

● giving myself a pat on the back

recommended links

@janesomebody on twitter

facebook promotion

Publisher's place

Agent's place

Amazon.com

exploring all of the options

posted by jane

Lorem ipsum dolor sit amet, consectetur adipiscing elit. Pellentesque sit amet tellus eu arcu malesuada pretium. Quisque id lectus vitae erat accumsan blandit. Cum sociis natoque penatibus et magnis dis parturient montes, nascetur ridiculus mus Class aptent taciti sociosqu ad litora torquent per conubia nostra, per inceptos himenaeos. Curabitur vel dui in tortor accumsan pharetra. Sed sed orci a justo porta consequat eget eu eram. Nulla ut mauris est. Duis dapibus urna vel massa pellentesque ultrices. Nunc urna erat, mollis eu ultrices ac, aliquam rutrum lacus.

Donec tempor nunc non purus rutrum tristique nec a nisl. Vivamus iaculis, dolor tempus aliquet fringilla, ipsum lectus imperdiet purus, vel rutrum ipsum nulla sit amet diam. Nunc placerat aliquet risus, eu cursus metus bibendum eget.Cras a elit vitae lorem auctor pellentesque. Curabitur nec ante sed sapien accumsan eleifend. Duis pellentesque dictum lorem eget sollicitudin. Donec id auctor dolor. Proin vel leo quis massa lacinia consequat.

Nam scelerisque quam quis tellus ullamcorper sit amet bibendum erat volutpat. Maecenas dolor enim, vulputate in dapibus ac, sodales in leo. Lorem ipsum dolor sit amet, consectetur adipiscing elit. Pellentesque nisi metus, posuere quis ultrices ut, blandit a diam. Etiam volutpat posuere lectus non cursus

comment | 0 comments | permalink | share this post

just another day in paradise or writing

posted by jane

Donec nec nunc vel magna lacinia egestas. Proin tempus tortor nec quam vulputate at mollis ipsum adipiscing. Pellentesque varius dictum ligula, at hendrerit purus fringilla non.

Fusce vel arcu ut erat placerat rutrum. Nam interdum sodales justo, sit amet commodo felis dictum sed.

comment | 0 comments | permalink | share this post

Now, let's dig a bit deeper into how you can manipulate layers to help you design. Make each layer behave independently of the others and therefore, manipulate what your final design will look like.

Locking layers

The idea of locking a layer—making it not editable—can be valuable when designing backgrounds, footers, or headers.

Time for action – locking a layer

Let's look at how you can lock a layer in Inkscape using the same design used previously. You can download the full project from `http://dl.dropbox.com/u/565455/` `exampleprojectlayout.svg`.

1. With the blog mockup from the pervious exercise open in Inkscape, open the **Layer** dialog. From the main menu, select **Layer** and then **Layers**. On the right side of your screen, the **Layers** dialog will be displayed and it will look something similar to the following screenshot:

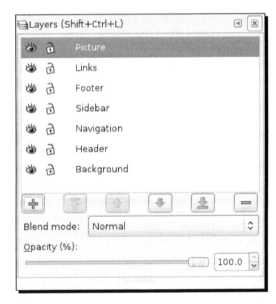

2. You will notice that each layer has icons to the left of the layer name. Go to the **Background** layer and click the **Lock** icon. You will see that once you click that icon, the lock now looks closed or locked, shown as follows:

This means that the **Background** layer can no longer be selected from the canvas, nor will any objects on this layer be able to be moved or edited.

3. For example, go to your canvas and try to select the **Background** objects. You will not be able to move this layer until you unlock it in the **Layer** dialog.

4. To unlock an item, click the **Lock** icon. Again, you will see the icon change to the unlock state, opening the layer objects for manipulation again.

What just happened?

In the previous example, we locked the header layer in the working document. This means we can't edit any objects on that layer, or move them to a new location on the canvas. Essentially, all items are locked into place.

This helps keep items that are "in place," stay in place while you work on the rest of the design. This can be especially handy when working in a series of designs where certain items will always stay in the same location.

Hiding layers

Another great feature when working with layers is to hide them. This means that while working with interim drafts of projects, you could create a layer for the first draft, and then another for the second—or you could even use layers for certain design elements that you want to turn on or off. All these are beneficial because the layer will hold objects' locations, but all you need to do is click a button to turn them on or off.

Time for action – hiding layers

To really show how powerful a feature hiding layers can be, let's walk through this example. We're going to change the design of the blog that we have been featuring in this entire chapter. In fact, we will change the navigation icons so that we can make two different designs:

1. With the blog mockup from the previous exercise open in Inkscape, reopen the **Layer** dialog if it is not open.

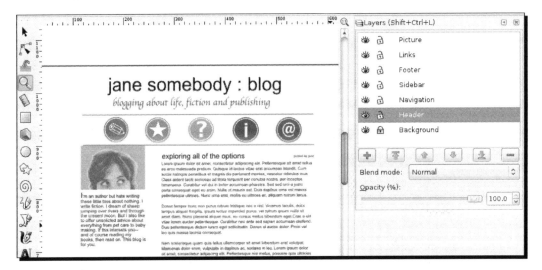

2. Select the **Navigation** layer.

3. Click the **Eye** icon to the left of the layer name.

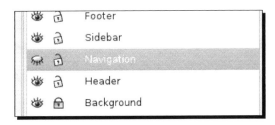

4. The eye will close and essentially hide all objects on that layer—as shown in the previous screenshot.

5. Now, you can create a new layer with the different navigation elements and make that viewable. This creates another design option to choose from. To do this, create the new layer by using the **Layer** dialog and the + sign or the *Shift + Ctrl + N* shortcut keys. Let's name the layer **Navigation Option 2**:

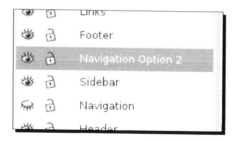

6. Make sure this layer remains selected and import some new navigational elements. Download the new icons from http://dl.dropbox.com/u/565455/ Newnavbuttons.zip.

7. Unzip the new icons to your desktop and drag-and-drop the files to your canvas (again, making sure the **Navigation Option 2** layer is active). You'll notice that since the original **Navigation** is still hidden, you don't see the icons:

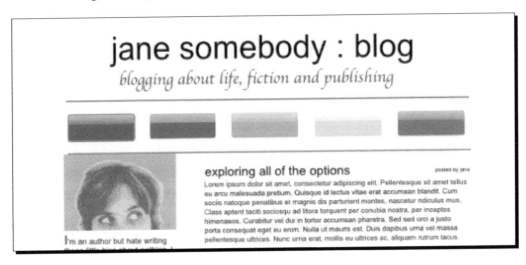

This is an ideal way to give certain design options to a client.

8. You can now save a PDF with the new navigation design. From the main menu, select **File | Save As | *.Portable Document Format**. You can leave all default values on in the PDF dialog to save the file.

9. Hide the layer **Navigation Option 2** (click the eye) and unhide the layer **Navigation** (click closed eye) to see the original design. Then save this version also as a PDF. From the main menu, select **File | Save As | *.Portable Document Format**. Of course, remember to give this new version a different PDF filename:

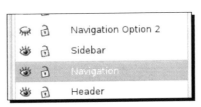

10. Also, saving this project as an Inkscscape SVG file would be beneficial, so all objects and this overall design can be edited later. From the main menu, select **File** and then select **Save**.

What just happened?

You hid one layer, created another layer, made a new design element, and learned how to switch between the two layers to show off two different designs.

In Inkscape, layer selection happens automatically when you select an object. This is different in comparison to many bitmap editors in the market, where you first have to select a layer to work on and then the object. With Inkscape, you can select any object and it will be immediately set as the current layer by Inkscape.

Have a go hero – show all but current layer

You can also hide or show all layers other than the current.

The following points explain how it is done:

1. Open the sample file that we created previously.

2. In the **Layer** dialog, right-click the layer name and choose **Show/hide other layers**.

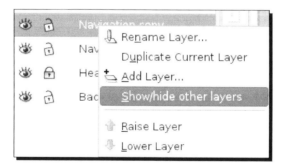

3. If the current layer is viewable (not hidden) it will hide all others except your working layer giving you access to that layer's content in isolation.

4. If the current layer is hidden, selecting the Show/hide other layers field, will unhide the current layer and then hide all others. Again, allowing you to work in only that layer with no other layers and their objects viewable.

Duplicating layers

Much like hiding layers, it can be very useful to duplicate certain layers so you can keep some of the same object attributes as the original (for example, opacity) or for the use of creating design mockups of multiple pages of a website, which have common elements. Also note that when you duplicate a layer it will duplicate all objects, including hidden or locked ones on any sub-layers as well. More information is given in the section *Time for action—nesting layers* later in this chapter in regard to sub-layers.

Time for action – duplicating layers

Here are the simple steps for duplicating a layer. We'll use the same example blog page as we have throughout this chapter.

1. Open the blog mockup from the previous exercises.

2. If your **Layer** dialog is open, you can right-click any layer and choose **Duplicate Current Layer.**

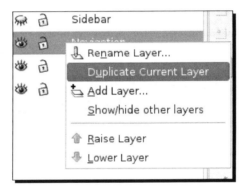

3. Alternatively, make sure the layer you want to duplicate is selected and from the main menu, choose **Layer** and then **Duplicate Current Layer**.

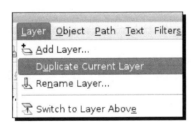

What just happened?

You have just created a literal duplicate of the layer on your screen to edit.

Note, however, that the duplicate layer is also right above the existing layer, so you may not be able to see which is selected. Look at the **Layer** dialog. It renames the duplicate layer: <original layer name> copy.

All objects on that layer are duplicated as well and will be placed on the canvas in the exact location of the original. If you move an object, you will see the other one below it.

Now you can move and/or edit objects as needed on this new layer without disturbing the original.

Arranging layers

You can also rearrange layers. Let's learn how to re-order the stack of layers, and move a layer to the top or bottom.

Time for action – moving layers

We're again going to use our blog design mockup file as an example. As the current screen stands, the layers don't overlap much—as all objects have a place. However, if we add a layer for a swirled background, it automatically places this layer on top, shown as follows:

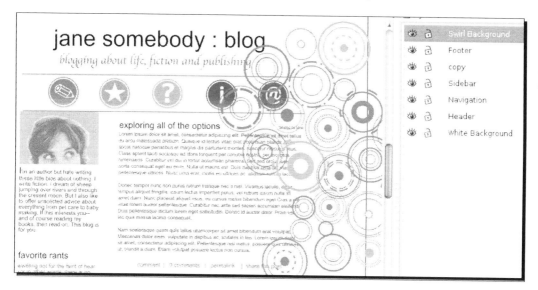

The following steps explain how to move it down to place it behind the main design:

1. Download a sample of the swirl background here: http://dl.dropbox.co/u/565455/ swirlbackground.svg.zip

2. In inkscape, in the layer dialog, add a new layer called Swirl Background.

3. Select the Swirl Background layer, and from the main menu choose File | Import. Select the Swirl Background SVG file.

4. Once the image is imported, select Swirl Background in the Layer dialog and use the arrow icon to move this layer just above the Background layer.

5. You could also use the move to bottom icon (just to the right of the move down icon)—since our background was set to white in the document properties.

   Now your canvas should look something similar to the following screenshot. Note, how the swirls are now behind the navigational buttons:

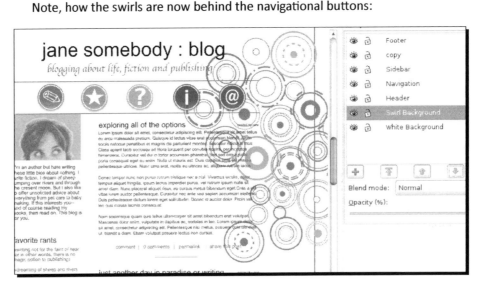

6. Make sure the **Swirl Background** layer is selected and move the **Opacity** bar at the bottom of the **Layer** dialog to **15%** (or type 15 in the **Opacity** field box). The opacity of the **Swirl Background** will change and you will now have a pattern-type background for this blog:

What just happened?

We took an additional design element, swirl objects, and made them part of the background in our blog design. We did this by creating a new **Swirl Background** layer and then moving that layer lower in the layer stack.

Then we decreased the opacity of that layer to 15 percent, so that it could be subtler in the design.

Pop quiz – background colors

1. What is the default background color of an Inkscape file?

    a. White

    b. Red

    c. Transparent

    d. Black

Time for action – nesting layers

You also have the option of nesting layers in Inkscape. Nesting is the idea of creating sublayers in Inkscape. You might want to do this if you want all sublayers to be virtually grouped with a parent layer and carry some of the parent layer's attributes.

Here's how we can create sublayers within the **Header** layer in our current project:

1. With the example project open, go to the **Layer** dialog (from the main menu, select **Layer** and then **Layers** or use the *Shift + Ctrl + L* keyboard shortcut to open it).

2. Right-click the **Header** layer and choose **Add Layer....**

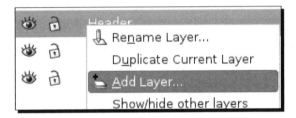

   The **Add Layer** dialog is displayed.

3. Type a new layer name into the **Layer name** field and then select **Position: As sublayer of current**.

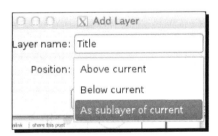

4. Click on **Add**.

5. The new sublayer displays as a nested layer beneath **Header**.

Unfortunately, at this time, there is no way to convert an existing Inkscape layer into a sublayer in the graphical interface. You can, however, go into the XML editor and make this change directly if needed. More information about sublayers can be seen in this online tutorial at `http://tavmjong.free.fr/INKSCAPE/MANUAL/html/XML.html`.

Also note, a sublayer cannot be moved outside of the parent layer it is under. Again, advanced use of the XML editor is needed to do this functionality.

What just happened?

We learned how to create nested sublayers in Inkscape.

Have a go hero – moving objects from one layer to another

Now that you have layers created—and objects on each layer—what if you want to move an object from one layer to another? Here's how it is done:

1. In an open Inkscape document with multiple layers, select an object.

2. If you want to move this object to the layer above the current layer, use **Layer | Move Selection to Layer Above** or the *Shift + PageUp* keyboard shortcut (for Macintosh users the keyboard shortcut is *Shift + Fn + Arrow up*).

3. If you want to move this object to the layer below the current layer, use **Layer | Move Selection to Layer Below** or the *Shift + PageDown* keyboard shortcut (for Macintosh users the keyboard shortcut is *Shift + Fn + Arrow down*).

Renaming layers

Sometimes while working within a document, you might find the need to rename a layer to a more descriptive name to the layer's contents.

Time for action – renaming a layer

The following steps explain how you would rename an existing layer in Inkscape:

1. Open an Inkscape document from previous exercises.

2. If your **Layer** dialog is open, you can right-click any layer and choose **Rename Layer**. Alternatively, from the main menu, select **Layer | Rename Layer....**

The **Rename Layer** dialog is displayed.

3. Type a new name for the layer and click **Rename**, as shown in the following screenshot:

What just happened?

We renamed an existing layer in Inkscape to the new name **body copy**.

Deleting layers

There are also times you might want to delete a layer. Just note that when you delete a layer if there are any objects on that layer, they will also be deleted.

Time for action – deleting a layer

1. Open an Inkscape document from a previous exercise.

2. If your **Layer** dialog is open, select the **Swirl Background** layer.

3. Then click the – icon as follows:

The selected layer is deleted.

4. If you decide you don't want to delete that layer, go to the main menu and select **Edit | Undo: Delete Layer** or use the *Ctrl + Z* keyboard shortcut to undo the last action:

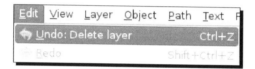

What just happened?

We deleted the layer named **Swirl Background** in our Inkscape document. We also learned that if we want to undo any action, we can use the **Undo** functionality in Inkscape.

Pop quiz – undo last action

1. What is the shortcut key combination to undo the last action in Inkscape?

    a. *Ctrl + Z*

    b. *Shift + Z*

    c. *Fn + Z*

    d. None of the above

Blend mode

In the **Layers** dialog, you may have noticed the **Blend mode** field, shown as follows:

This field is a shortcut to apply the Blend filter to an entire layer. This means that if any objects overlap on the selected layers, Inkscape will do a pixel-by-pixel blend of the two objects. Here's what each **Blend mode** option means:

- **Normal**: No filter added to the layer
- **Multiply**: Objects on the top layer filter the light from the objects on the bottom-most layer. (or from the background if a bottom object does not exist)
- **Screen**: The top objects add light to the bottom object
- **Darken**: The objects on top darken the bottom objects
- **Lighten**: The top objects lighten the bottom objects

If at any time you return the **Blend mode** back to **Normal**, the blend filter disappears.

Time for action – using Blend mode

Let's add in a **Multiply** blend filter to two simple objects as an example:

1. Open a new document in Inkscape.

2. Use the **Circle/Ellipse** tool and create one red circle and one yellow circle, shown as follows:

3. Now move the yellow circle so it overlaps the red circle:

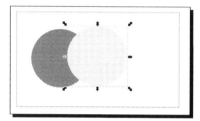

4. Open the **Layers** dialog and go to the **Blend mode** drop-down menu. Select **Multiply** as follows:

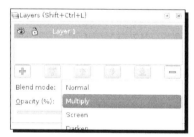

The two objects combine as if light were shining through both. The red and yellow objects—where they overlap—display orange, shown as follows:

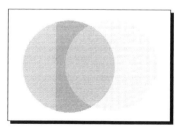

5. If you now change the **Blend mode** back to **Normal**, the two objects now go back to being normal, or just simply overlapping.

What just happened?

We learned how to adjust the **Blend mode** between layers. We took two example objects (circles in this case) and gave them the **Multiply** blend. Then we learned how to turn the blend back to **Normal** mode.

Summary

We learned essentially everything there is to know about **Layers** in this chapter. We discussed how to create new layers, lock them, hide them, nest sublayers, and even how to duplicate and arrange layers. We even spent a bit of time discussing the **Blend mode** feature when using layers—which can be a helpful tool to get text or object effects. Up next, we are going to learn about building objects.

6

Building Objects

This chapter is all about objects. We'll learn about what objects are and how Inkscape interprets them, how to change object features, change fill and stroke, grouping objects, combining objects, and how to best use the masking and clipping features.

Details in this chapter include:

- ◆ Working with objects
- ◆ Fill and Stroke
- ◆ Grouping
- ◆ Clipping and masking

Working with objects

Objects in Inkscape are any shapes that make up your overall drawing. This means that any text, path, or shape that you create is essentially an object.

Let's start by making a simple object and then changing some of its attributes.

Time for action – creating a simple object

Inkscape can create predefined shapes that are part of the SVG standard. These include rectangles/squares, circles/ellipses/arcs, stars, polygons, and spirals. To create any of these shapes, you can select items from the toolbar:

However, you can also create more freehand-based objects as well. Let's look at how we can create a simple freehand triangle:

1. Select the Bezier tool:

2. Click once where you want the first corner and then move the mouse/pointer to the next corner. A node appears with the click and then a freehand line:

3. When you have the length of the first side of the triangle estimated, click for the second corner:

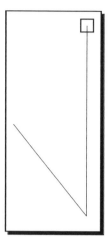

4. Move the mouse to form the second side and click for the third corner:

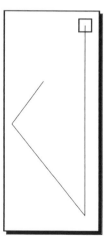

5. Move the mouse back to the first corner node and click it to form the triangle, shown as follows:

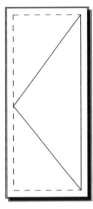

6. Now save the file. From the main menu, select **File** and then **Save**. We will use this triangle to build a graphic later in this book, so choose a location to save so that you will know where to find the file.

7. Now that the basic triangle is saved, let's also experiment with how we can manipulate the shape itself and/or the shape's position on the canvas. Let's start with manipulating the triangle.

8. Select the triangle and drag a handle to a new location. You have essentially skewed the triangle, as shown in the following diagram:

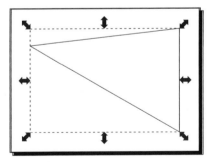

9. To change the overall shape of the triangle, select the triangle, then click the **Edit path by Nodes** tool (or press *F2*):

10. Now the nodes of the triangle are displayed as follows:

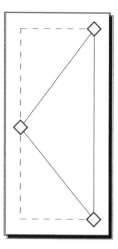

11. Nodes are points on a path that define the path's shape. Click a node and you can drag it to another location to manipulate the triangle's overall shape as follows:

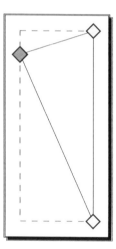

12. Double-click between two nodes to add another node and change the shape:

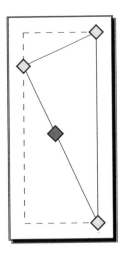

13. If you decide that you don't want the extra node, click it (the node turns red), press *Delete* on your keyboard and it disappears.

14. You can also use the control bar to add, delete, or manipulate the path/shape and nodes:

15. If you want to change the position of the shape on the canvas by choosing the Select tool in the toolbox, click and drag the shape and move it where you need it to be.

16. Change the size of the shape by also choosing the Select tool from the toolbox, clicking and holding the edge of the shape at the handle (small square or circles at edges), and dragging it outward to grow larger or inward to shrink until the shape is of the desired size.

17. You can also rotate an object. Choose the Select tool from the toolbox and single-click the shape until the nodes turn to arrows with curves (this might require you to click the object a couple of times). When you see the curved arrow nodes, click-and-drag on a corner node to rotate the object until it is rotated and positioned correctly.

18. No need to save this file again after we have manipulated it—unless you want to reference this new version of the triangle for future projects. But we will revisit the original triangle shape in *Chapter 7, Using Paths*.

What just happened?

We created a free-form triangle and saved it for a future project. We also manipulated the shape in a number of ways—used the nodes to change the skew of the overall shape, added nodes to change the shape completely, and also how to move the shape around on the canvas.

Fill and Stroke

As you've already noticed, when creating objects in Inkscape they have color associated with them. You can fill an object with a color as well as give the object an outline or stroke. This section will explain how to change these characteristics of an object in Inkscape.

Fill and Stroke dialog

You can use the **Fill and Stroke** dialog from the main menu to change the fill colors of an object.

Time for action – using the Fill and Stroke dialog

Let's open the dialog and get started:

1. Open your triangle Inkscape file again and select the triangle.

2. From the main menu, choose **Object | Fill and Stroke** (or use the *Shift + Ctrl + F* keyboard shortcut).

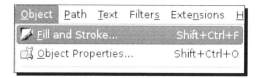

3. The **Fill and Stroke** dialog appears on the right-hand side of your screen. Notice it has three tabs: **Fill**, **Stroke paint**, and **Stroke style**, as shown in the following screenshot:

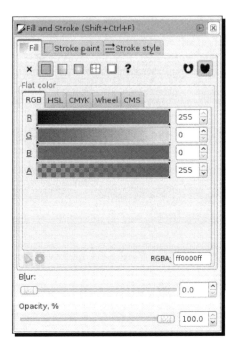

4. Select the **Fill** tab (if not already selected). Here are the options for fill:

   ❑ **Type of fill**: The buttons below the **Fill** tab allow you to select the type of fill you would like to use. No fill (the button with the X), flat color, linear or radial gradients. In the previous example screenshot, the flat fill button is selected.

   ❑ **Color picker**: Another set of tabs below the type of the fill area are presented; **RGB**, **CMYK**, **HSL**, and **Wheel**. You can use any of these to choose a color. The most intuitive option is **Wheel** as it allows you to visually see all the colors and rotate a triangle to the color of your choice, as shown in the following screenshot:

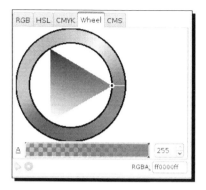

- ❏ Once a color is chosen, then the exact color can be seen in various values on the other color picker tabs.

- ❏ **Blur**: Below the color area, you also have an option to blur the object's fill. This means that if you move the sliding lever to the right, the blur of the fill will move outward. See the following diagram for examples of an object without and with blur:

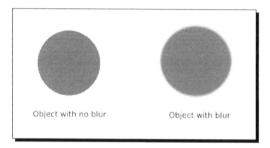

- ❏ **Opacity**: Lastly, there is the opacity slider. By moving this slider to the right you will give the object an alpha of opacity setting making it a bit more transparent. The following diagram demonstrates opacity:

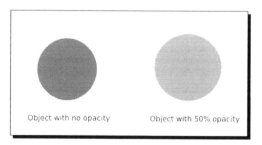

5. In the **Fill and Stroke** dialog, if you select the **Stroke paint** tab, you will notice it looks very much like the **Fill** tab. You can remove the stroke (outline) of the object, set the color, and determine if it is a flat color or gradient:

6. In the last tab, **Stroke style** is where you can most notably set the width of the stroke:

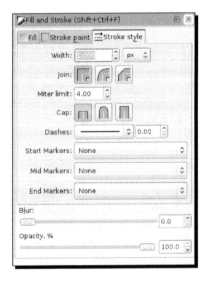

7. You can also use this tab to determine what types of corners or joins an object has (round or square corners) and how the end caps of the border look like.

8. The **Dashes** field gives options for the stroke line type, as shown in the following screenshot:

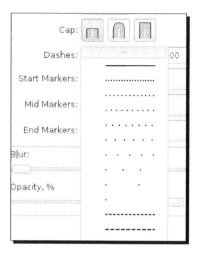

9. Start, Mid, and End Markers allow you to add end points to your strokes, as follows:

10. For our triangle object, use the **Fill** tab and choose a green color, no stroke, and 100 percent opacity:

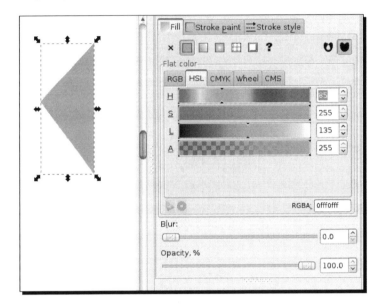

What just happened?

You learned where to open the **Fill and Stroke** dialog, adjust the fill of an object, use blur and opacity, and how to change the stroke color and weights of the stroke line.

Next, let's learn other ways to change the fill and stroke options.

Color palette bar

You can also use the color palette bar to change fill color:

Time for action – using the color palette

Let's learn all the tips and tricks for using the color palette bar:

1. From the palette bar, click a color and drag it from the palette onto the object to change its fill, as shown in the following diagram:

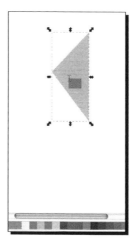

2. You can also change an object and the stroke color in a number of other ways:

- ❑ Select an object on the canvas and then click a color box in the palette to immediately set the fill of an object.
- ❑ Select an object on the canvas and then right-click a color box in the palette. A popup menu appears with options to set the fill (and stroke).
- ❑ If you hold the *Shift* key and drag a color box onto an object, it changes the stroke color.
- ❑ *Shift* + left-click a color box to immediately set the stroke color.

 Note, you can use the scroll bar just below the viewable color swatches on the color palette to scroll right to see even more color choices.

What just happened?

You learned how to change the fill and stroke color of an object by using the color swatches on the color palette bar on the main screen of Inkscape.

Dropper

Yet another way to change the fill or stroke of an object is to use the dropper:

Let's learn how to use it.

Time for action – using the dropper tool

Open an Inkscape file with objects on the canvas or create a quick object to try this out:

1. Select an object on the canvas.

2. Select the dropper tool from the toolbar or use the shortcut key *F7*.

3. Then click anywhere in the drawing with that tool that has the color you want to choose. The chosen color will be assigned to the selected object's fill. Alternatively, use *Shift* + click to set the stroke color.

4. Be aware of the tool control bar and the dropper tool controls, shown as follows:

5. The two buttons affect the opacity of the object, especially if it is different than the 100% setting.

   - If **Pick** is disabled, then the color as chosen by the dropper looks exactly like it is on screen

   - If **Pick** is enabled and **Assign** is disabled, then the color picked by the dropper is one that the object would have if its opacity was 100%

   - If **Pick** is enabled and **Assign** is enabled, then the color and opacity are both copied from the picked object

What just happened?

By using the dropper tool, you learned how to change a color of another object on the screen.

Pop quiz – changing Fill and Stroke

TRUE OR FALSE: No matter what way you use to change fill and stroke of an object in Inkscape, it all has the same outcome for the object on your canvas.

Grouping

You can combine several objects into what we call a group. The group then, can be moved or transformed (made larger/smaller) as if it were one object.

Time for action – grouping objects

When grouping objects, there is no limit to the number of objects that can be grouped together. You can also take multiple groups and group them together as well. Let's start with a simple example of how to group objects:

1. Open an Inkscape document and draw separate objects to create the shape of a sun as follows:

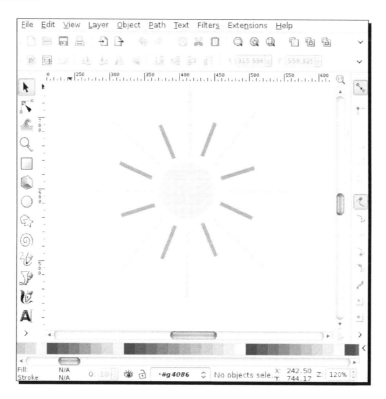

2. Now select all the objects on your screen. Click the select tool and then click and drag a bounding box around all objects that you want in the group or press the *Ctrl + A* key and select all objects on the canvas:

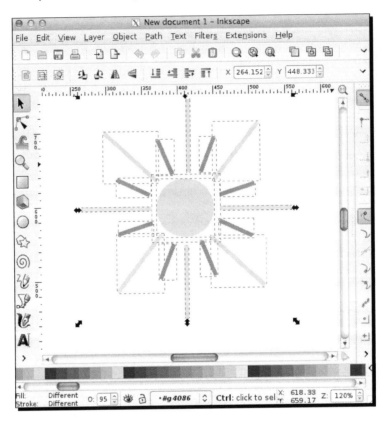

3. Once all the objects are selected, from the main menu select **Object | Group** or use the *Ctrl + G* shortcut keys, as shown in the following screenshot:

You'll notice the bounding box that was once around each individual object has now bound around the entire group of objects. You'll also notice in the status bar that a group is selected and the number of objects it contains (group of <x> objects in layer <layer name>).

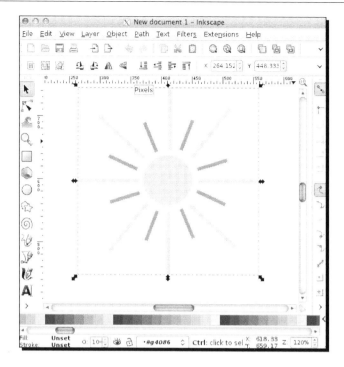

4. Now you can select the group and move it on the canvas. Notice, all of the objects move as one:

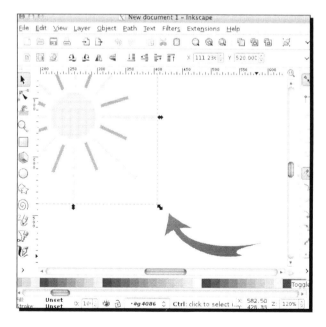

5. You can also transform the object by dragging any corner node to make the group of objects smaller or bigger. You can even drag those handles and skew and rotate the group of objects as follows:

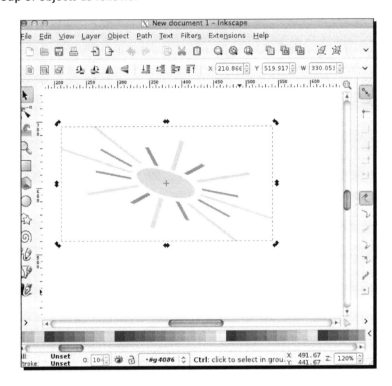

6. To add additional objects to this group, double-click the group itself then draw or paste the new object to be included.

To ungroup, select the group and then from the main menu select **Object | Ungroup** (or use the shortcut keys *Ctrl + U*). If you have grouped more than one group, ungrouping will only "disconnect" the topmost level of grouping; you'll need to ungroup repeatedly to keep ungrouping objects.

7. If you want to edit an object within a group, you don't have to ungroup it. Just press the *Ctrl* key and click that object and it will be selected and editable. Alternatively, select the node tool and click the individual object within a group for editing.

What just happened?

You were able to group several objects and then manipulate that group of objects as one—moving, transforming, and editing it. We even discussed a little trick about editing individual objects within a group.

Pop quiz – shortcut keys to quickly ungroup items

1. What is the shortcut key combination for quickly ungrouping items?

    a. *Shift + G + U*

    b. *Ctrl + G*

    c. *Shift + G*

    d. *Ctrl + U*

Clipping and masking

Another way of joining objects is to use clips and masks. These features are used to determine which parts of an object are visible. **Clips** define what areas of another object are fully visible. Technically speaking, Inkscape takes the top object's path in and clips all the paths below it (in the selection) to the shape of the top path.

When you use a **mask** it visually crops objects with transparent areas to become fully transparent in the masked object, white areas become fully opaque, and all other colors translate into different levels of opacity in the masked object. To make sure this is clear, we'll do a few exercises.

Time for action – clipping objects

Let's build out our triangle object and create a tree that has a pattern of leaves in it:

1. Open your triangle Inkscape file.

2. Use the Bezier tool and create a rectangular shape below your triangle, as shown in the following diagram:

3. Remember if you don't get the lines exactly right the first time, select the **Edit Paths by Nodes** tool and adjust by dragging the nodes to the appropriate locations.

4. Draw another rectangular object below the previous one, as shown in the following diagram:

5. And draw the final rectangle below the last one as follows:

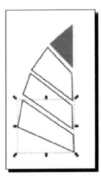

6. Now we are going to focus on making the left sides of the three rectangular objects more rounded and smooth. Select the first rectangle and choose the **Edit Paths by Nodes** tool.

7. Add a node on the left side of that rectangular object:

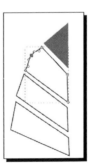

8. Select the smooth node option from the control bar:

9. Your left side will now become a curve, as shown in the following diagram:

10. Repeat, adding a node and smoothing the left side of each of the remaining two rectangles as follows:

11. On the bottom rectangle, add another node in the middle of the bottom side and smooth it so it has a more rounded side to it, as shown in the following diagram:

12. Now it is time to adjust the color and stroke of each of the objects on the canvas. Move the color palette bar scroll bar to the right to get to a set of green colors as follows:

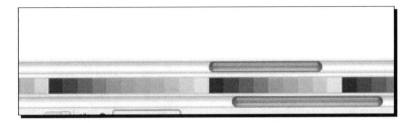

13. Select the top triangle and choose a light color green for it:

14. Select each of the rectangles and give an increasingly darker green color to them as follows:

15. Now select all objects on the canvas (*Ctrl + A*) and remove the stroke:

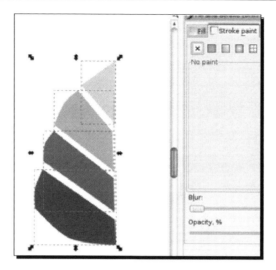

16. With all of the objects still selected on the canvas, create a duplicate of them. From the main menu select **File | Duplicate** (or use the *Ctrl + D* shortcut keys).

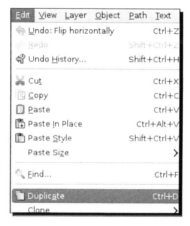

17. Click the flip horizontally button:

18. Move the objects so they mirror the original shapes, as shown in the following diagram:

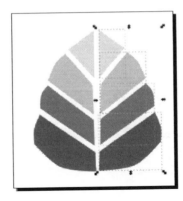

19. Add a long vertical rectangle at the bottom for the leaf stem:

20. Again, select all objects on the screen by pressing *Ctrl + A* and group them so they become one object. From the main menu select **Object | Group** or use the *Ctrl + G* shortcut keys. You have created one leaf!

21. Select your leaf, press the *Shift* key, and then drag the handle of the bounding box inward to scale your leaf smaller.

22. With the leaf still selected, from the main menu choose, **Edit | Clone | Create Tiled Clones...** as shown in the following screenshot:

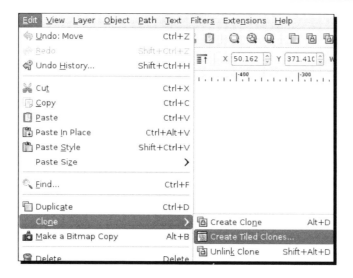

23. From the **Clone** dialog, for **Rows, columns:** adjust to **10 x 10** and click **Create**, as shown in the following screenshot:

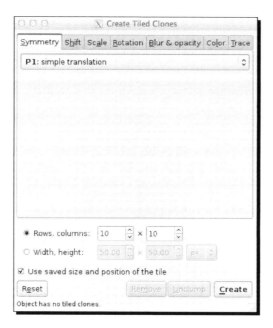

24. Your canvas will now have a pattern/grid of leaves on it:

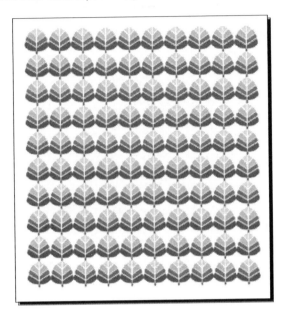

25. Press *Ctrl + A* to select all of the leaves and then use the *Ctrl + G* shortcut keys to group them.

26. Use the Bezier tool and create a simple triangle tree shape, as shown in the following diagram:

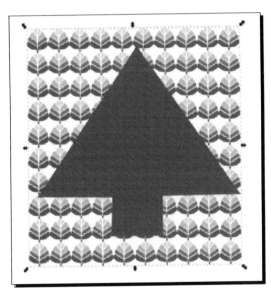

27. Make sure that the basic tree you just created (that will be used as a clip or mask) overlaps the others. You can use the *Ctrl + Page Up* keys to ensure an object is the topmost object.

28. Press *Ctrl + A* to select all objects on your canvas.

29. In the main menu select **Object | Clip | Set**, as shown in the following screenshot:

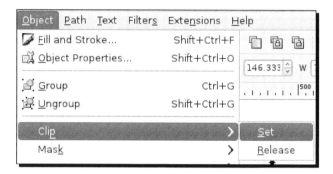

30. You can see how the top object becomes the shape of the object with the bottom object peeking through. Note, if you select three objects (instead of grouping) and perform a clip, you'll end up with two separate clipped objects:

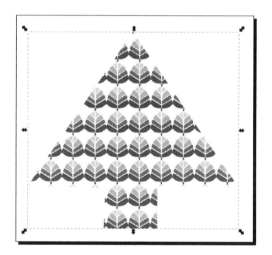

 Just like in a group, if you double-click a clip, you will be able to select and edit the objects within it.

31. To edit the actual clip (or mask), you will have to release it first. From the main menu select **Object | Clip | Release**.

What just happened?

We took some objects, built a leaf object, cloned it to make a pattern, and used that to create a clipping mask. We even learned a few details about how to edit objects within the clip as well as releasing.

Time for action – masking objects

Here are some quick steps to see what a mask will look like:

1. Use the same objects in an open Inkscape document as in the previous example. This time, however, let's make the background leaves black and the tree in front a grayscale color as follows:

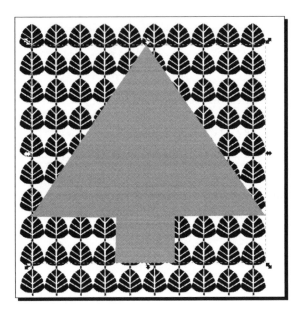

2. Press *Ctrl + A* to select all objects on your canvas.

3. In the main menu select **Object | Mask | Set**.

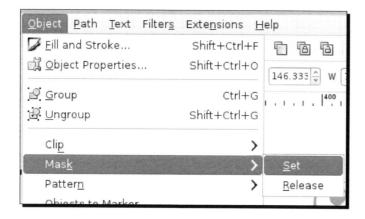

4. In this result, the top object also becomes the overall shape, while the bottom peeks through. However, you will notice the degrees of grayscale setting over the entire object now. Masking depends only on grayscale. Thus, when using white, the objects below will be fully visible; when using black, the objects below will be fully blocked; and any gray level in between, the objects will be partially masked as in our example:

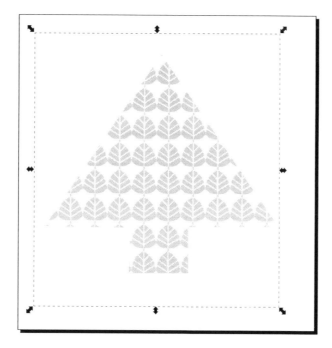

Just like in a group, if you double-click a clip, you will be able to select and edit the objects within it.

5. One other item to note here is that the resulting masked object will have a bounding box that will be as large as the largest object, which will make it hard to scale and align in some design situations.

6. To edit the actual clip (or mask), you will have to release it first. From the main menu, select **Object | Mask | Release**.

What just happened?

This time we created a mask and learned how to edit and release it in Inkscape.

Summary

You should be ready to move forward and learn even more about creating paths into complex shapes. We spent most of this chapter learning about the nuances of objects in Inkscape; how to build the predefined shapes and then how to combine and alter them using fills, strokes, clips, masks, and more. Now, we will learn about paths and how to manipulate them.

7
Using Paths

This chapter will focus on using paths. Paths are a critical element to Inkscape. We will focus on learning what paths are, working with them in Inkscape, and transforming, combining, and placing paths.

The following will be covered in the chapter:

- ◆ Working with paths
- ◆ Transforming objects into paths
- ◆ Using stroke to paths
- ◆ Path options
- ◆ Combining and breaking paths
- ◆ Path placement

Working with paths

As stated previously, vector graphics themselves are made up of paths. Paths can be used to create unique text styling when tracing other images like photographs, and when building icons, buttons, and logos. By adding and manipulating nodes, you can transform simple paths into elaborate illustrations.

The most common tool used to create paths in Inkscape is the **Bezier tool** and this is what will be used in most of the examples seen throughout this chapter. You can also use the Pencil (Freehand) and Calligraphy tools to create paths. All of these tools are found in the toolbox.

Before we get started, here are some key items to remember when using the Bezier tool when creating paths:

- To start creating a path with the Bezier tool, click each spot you want a node to appear in
- A single click creates a straight line and a sharp node creates a "corner"
- To create a smooth node or a curve--click, hold and drag your cursor to create the curved/smooth node
- Double-click to finish the path (for an open object)
- To "close" a path, double-click on the starting node
- Also, when you are drawing lines, the green lines are the completed segments and the red lines are those that you are still making

Let's jump in and start by learning how to build multiple paths into an interesting object. In the following examples, we will build a caricature of a woman's face. Each exercise will build on the next until we have a full image.

Time for action – using the Bezier tool

To begin, we will use the Bezier tool to create a woman's face shape:

1. Open a new document in Inkscape.

2. Now select the Bezier tool from the toolbox bar:

3. Using a series of straight paths, using single-clicks to create nodes, create a head shape, similar to the one shown in the following image:

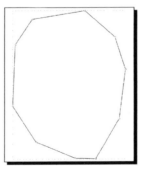

4. Make sure to close the path by double-clicking on the first node when complete.

5. Select the head object and choose the **Edit Paths by Nodes** tool:

All nodes on the object appear in a gray color.

From the main menu, choose **Edit | Select All** or use the *Ctrl + A* keyboard shortcut to select all nodes.

6. From the control bar, select the make selected nodes smooth icon:

All of the "angles" on your head shape will become smooth and have rounded corners:

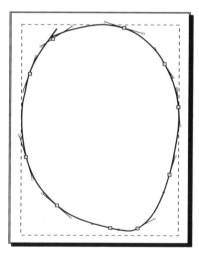

7. Double-click a node to adjust its position (if needed). The node turns into a red square when it is "active" for you to edit its location. Now click-and-drag it to a new location.

As shown in the following image, the lower or chin portion of the head was adjusted to make it a bit more rounded. All of this is done by double-clicking the lower two nodes and moving their positions:

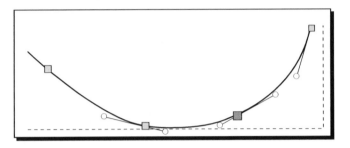

 If, for any reason, you move a node and an undesired effect results, you can always undo the last node movement by using the keyboard shortcut *Ctrl + Z* or from the main menu, select **Edit | Undo**.

8. You can also adjust the curves of each node/path by moving the circular handles on each node. Select the node you would like to adjust, and instead of clicking-and-dragging the node, click-and-drag a handle (it will also turn red when active) to a new location.

You can also adjust the curve placement by moving the node along the path in either direction.

On the example, the node and its respective handles on the left side of the face were adjusted to make the face shape a bit more round:

The shape of the face should now look similar to the following image:

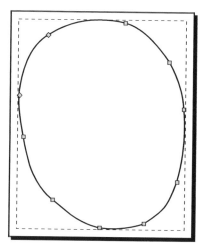

9. Select the face object and choose a white fill from the color palette.

10. To work more easily with the facial features, let's lock this layer and create a new one. Press the shortcut keys: *Shift + Ctrl + L* to open the **Layers** dialog.

11. Press the lock key for Layer 1.

12. Create a new layer for the eyes. Press the + button in the **Layers** dialog. Name the layer **Features** and click **Add**.

13. Within the new layer, select the Bezier tool and create a diamond-like eye shape to start. In the following example, use four nodes (four clicks) to create this shape:

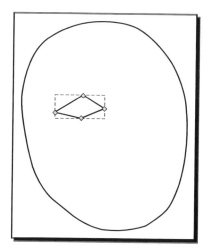

14. Again, click the **Edit Paths by Nodes** tool to edit the nodes of the eye object.

15. Select the top and bottom nodes of the eye object (use the *Shift* + click to select both nodes) and click the make selected nodes smooth icon to smooth the node angles:

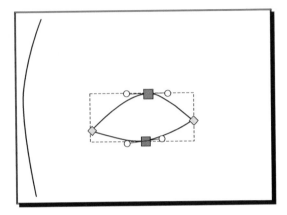

16. To stylize the eye, let's pull the left node out to create a point as follows:

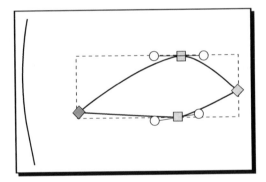

17. From the main menu, select **Edit | Duplicate** (or use the *Ctrl + D* keyboard shortcut).

18. Click the flip object horizontally button on the control bar:

19. Place the right eye so that the middle edges are along the same horizontal plane. However, note, this horizontal line will be at a slight angle to accommodate for the tilting of the face:

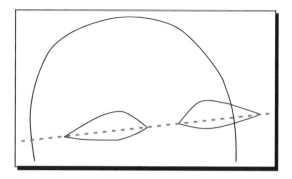

20. Select the face object from Layer 1 (if you locked Layer 1, remember to unlock it first from the **Layers** dialog).

21. From the main menu, select **Edit | Duplicate** (or use the *Ctrl + D* keyboard shortcut).

22. Press *Shift + Page Up* (for Mac computers, press *Shift + Fn +* up arrow) to move the face object to the **Features** layer. Your screen should look similar to the following image:

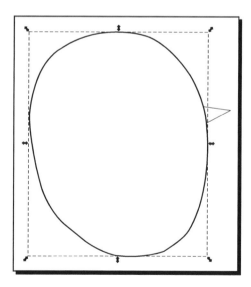

23. Hold the *Shift* key and also select the "tail" of the eye that is seen from underneath the duplicate face object.

24. From the main menu, select **Object | Clip | Set**:

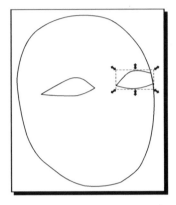

25. Hold the *Shift* key and select the other eye object. From the color palette, click black to fill both objects' color to black:

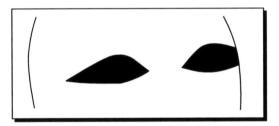

26. Click the Bezier tool and create a diamond shape, similar to what is shown in the following image, for the lips:

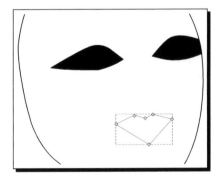

Notice, this shape has six nodes. These were created with six clicks (double-click at the end to close the object).

If you had missed adding a node to form the lips, there is no need to delete the object and start over. You can double-click on any path to add a new node. Also, if you added too many nodes, you can always select the extra nodes and press the *Delete* key to erase them.

27. Select the lips and click the **Edit Paths by Nodes** tool to edit the nodes of the lip object.

28. Select the top two nodes and bottom node of the lip object (use *Shift* + click to select all three nodes) and click the make selected nodes smooth icon to smooth the node angles as follows:

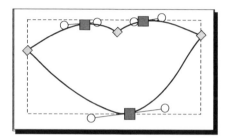

29. Now move the nodes accordingly to adjust the lips to the right size and proportion. Notice, in the following example, the left and right nodes were pulled outward to broaden the lips. Also the two top rounded nodes were pulled left and right respectively to move the curve of the lips outward and the handles of both curves were used to get the appropriate curves of the lips:

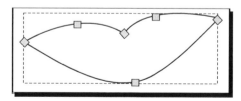

30. Select red color from the color palette to fill the lip objects with color.

31. Right-click the stroke color from the status bar and choose none to remove the stroke from the lip object as well:

32. If you made it this far, save your file so we can move on to the next step in the process—creating the hair. From the main menu, select **File | Save**.

What just happened?

We started a new project: a stylized image of a woman's face. This project, so far, was created mostly using the Bezier tool. In fact, we used that as the base tool for creating every object on this canvas so far.

We learned the Bezier tool basics—what a single-click versus a double-click accomplishes (creating nodes on a path versus closing/ending a path), how to make a straight versus curved node, how to adjust node placements, add new nodes, and how to delete nodes.

We created the very basics of a face at this point in the project. Now we will move into the second part of the project where we will add hair to this project. In doing so, we will continue to use the Bezier tool, but also add in the use of spiros and swirls.

Pop quiz – remove the last node movement

1. If, for any reason, you move a node and an undesired effect results—what can you do to "undo" it?

    a. Use the keyboard shortcut *Ctrl + Z*

    b. From the main menu select **Edit** and **Undo**

    c. Delete the entire path

    d. Both a and b

Transforming objects into paths

In Inkscape, any shape, text, or object that you created can be converted to a shape. Don't be fooled when it doesn't look like anything has happened because any capabilities that you had before (dragging corner nodes to scale larger, editing text, rounding corners on a square) can be lost, but now, you would be able to edit the object's nodes just like any other path (such as in our previous example).

Stroke to paths

You can convert the outline or stroke of any object and convert that to a path. Select an object with a stroke set—then from the main menu, select **Path | Stroke to Path**.

Again, the overall appearance on the canvas does not change, but how you can manipulate the object. Take a look at the number of nodes before this spiro was converted into a path, versus after:

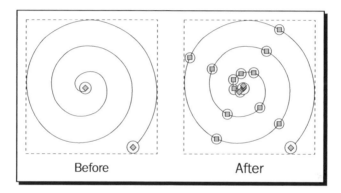

Before   After

Time for action – creating spiros and swirls

Let's open our previous project of the woman's face and give her some hair. In doing so, we will use the Bezier tool and the spiral object in Inkscape (as shown previously), convert it to a path, and manipulate it to create curls as follows:

1. Open the woman's face project we've been working on.

2. Press the shortcut keys: *Shift + Ctrl + L* to open the **Layers** dialog.

3. Create a new layer for the hair object(s). Press the + button in the **Layers** dialog. Name the layer **Hair** and click **Add**.

4. Select the Bezier tool and create a general shape for her hair, as shown in the following image:

A few items to remember here are that you can add nodes, delete them, move and adjust them, so that you get a general hair shape that you like.

5. Now let's work some more with the nodes on the hair. You can select specific nodes (use *Shift* + click to select multiple nodes at the same time) and click the make selected nodes smooth icon to smooth the node angles. Also, just as in the previous exercise, feel free to move nodes and handles as needed for your desired effect.

6. You can also work with a number of smaller paths and then combine them as you need to. Important tools to remember are the join selected nodes, break path at selected nodes, join selected end nodes with segment, and delete segment between two non-endpoint nodes tools—all found on the control bar:

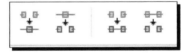

These buttons allow you to connect (or disconnect) two separate paths you have created with the Bezier tool.

7. For example let's break apart nodes near the neckline area and combine them so it looks like she has full flowing hair across her neck. Use *Shift* + click to select the nodes you want to break apart and then click the break paths and selected node button on the control bar as follows:

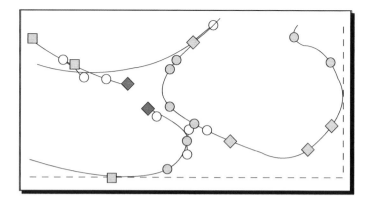

8. Perform the same steps for two nodes on the right-hand side hair as well:

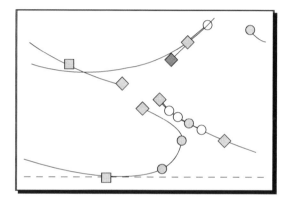

9. Now select the top node from the left-hand side and the top node from the right and click the join selected end nodes with segment button. The nodes are joined, as shown in the following image:

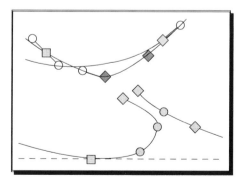

10. Repeat the process for the remaining two "open" nodes.

11. Give the hair some color as we work the shape a bit more. From the bottom color palette, choose black to fill this object with color and to give a more realistic view of the final project, as shown in the following image:

12. Continue to delete, move, and adjust nodes again to get a look of full hair at the neck because next we will be adding in some curls:

13. Select the spiral tool icon from the toolbox bar:

14. In the control bar, change the **Turns**, **Divergence**, and **Inner radius** settings to your liking. For our purposes, we'll change them, as shown in the following screenshot, to create a smooth curve:

15. Now, draw the spiral on your canvas outside of your face objects for now:

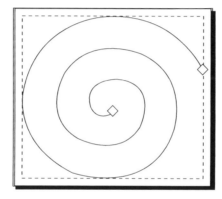

16. If you want to adjust the spiral, select the end nodes tool and start changing it to your liking:

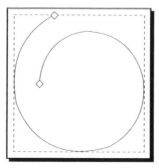

17. Click twice until you see the rotation handles. Float your mouse pointer over the tiny cross hair (center of rotation) in the center of the object. Now use *Shift* + drag to place the center of rotation above the location where the inner path ends, as shown in the following image:

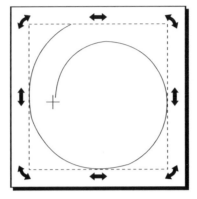

18. Now we need to change the spiral object to a path. From the main menu, select **Path** and then **Object to Path**.

19. Next, from the main menu, select **Edit** and then **Duplicate**. We now have two spirals (one on top of another).

20. Choose the selector tool and then double-click the top duplicated spiral so the rotation handles appear, and rotate it just a bit as follows:

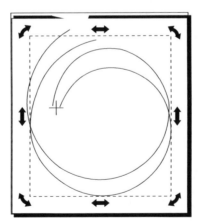

21. Now click the original spiral, so that it is selected and scale it to a size that makes the swirl interesting. It might look something like the following image:

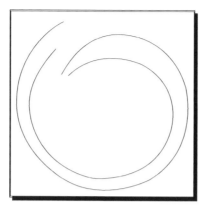

22. Now still with the selector tool, select both spirals (hold the *Shift* key and click-and-drag a bounding box over both spirals).

23. From the main menu, select **Path** and then combine.

24. Press the *F2* key to switch to the **Edit Path by Nodes** tool and then select both outer end nodes and click the join selected end nodes with a new segment button as follows:

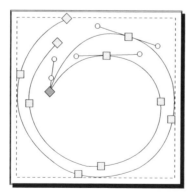

This joins the two nodes.

25. Do this with any other end nodes that aren't joined, smooth out any areas of the spiral to make it look more appealing, and delete any overlapping or crossovers of the lines:

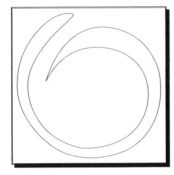

26. Click white on the color palette bar to add a fill color to this spiral and remove the stroke.

27. Now drag it onto the hair of your image as follows:

28. Scale, rotate, skew, mode/delete nodes, and/or duplicate the swirls or other similar objects to use them as other "curls" and "highlights" in the hair object.

29. Again, adjust nodes in the hair as needed to achieve a pleasing effect for your image. See the following image for a version of this project. Note, all highlights and curls in the hair were adjusted, duplicated versions of the first. Nodes were deleted, added, and moved to create the others:

30. From the main menu, select **File | Save** to save this project for future use and reference.

What just happened?

We spent even more time using paths. This time we started again with a Bezier tool and created a shape for the hair, but we then joined nodes with additional segments. Then we used a spiral object and converted it into a path to manipulate it and use it as curls within our project's hair.

Next up, we will work with text and convert it to a path.

Object to Path

To convert an object, we just select it and then from the main menu, choose **Path | Object to Path** or the *Shift + Ctrl + C* keyboard shortcut.

Note the following when you convert any text to a path:

- ◆ The text becomes non-editable as a normal object.
- ◆ The result will be a group of paths (one path for each letter). Then you can manipulate each letter by dragging nodes and editing the shape of each one individually.
- ◆ You can always ungroup the letters. On the main menu, select **Object | Ungroup**.

Let's convert an object to a path and then demonstrate how we can edit it differently now that it is a path.

Time for action – Object to Path

We'll add stylized text to our current project of the woman's face to illustrate how to use the **Object to Path** functionality and how we can further manipulate the text when we use this feature:

1. Open your previous Inkscape project.

2. Press the shortcut keys: *Shift + Ctrl + L* to open the **Layers** dialog if it is not already open.

3. Create a new layer for the hair object(s). Press the + button in the **Layers** dialog. Name the layer: **Text** and click **Add**.

>
> **Locking layers**
> To prevent accidentally selecting other objects, lock all other layers except the one you are currently working on. In this case, lock all layers except the **Text** layer.

4. In the **Add Layer**, select the create and edit text button from the toolbox:

5. Click on the canvas and type the word: SMILE:

6. Now we are going to convert the text to a path. From the main menu, choose **Path | Object to path**.

   Now when you select the word, the bounding box has changed and you can only select individual letters as follows:

7. You can manipulate or add effects to individual letters, or scale and transform each letter differently.

    In the following example for the S and E, the outside nodes were "pulled" into a smile.

    The letters MIL were stretched to larger sizes based on the placement. For the M and I, we also moved the outside nodes to make the letters wider. The letter I also had its fill color changed to red and a drop shadow added (**Filters | Shadows and Glows | Drop Shadow**):

8. From the main menu, select **File | Save** to save this project for future use and reference.

What just happened?

We created some sample text within our current project and then converted the text into paths. Once converted into paths, there were examples given on what you can do to each letter.

Pop quiz – paths

1. What can you convert to paths?

    a. Text

    b. Shapes

    c. Objects

    d. All of the above

Path options

Paths can be combined in a number of ways:

Here's what each of these joining options mean:

- **Union**: When you make a union of one or more paths, a new path is created that contains all areas of other parts. For example, the arrow we created earlier in this book joined all paths into one object.

- **Difference**: When you complete the difference between two paths or objects—the top path is removed from that of the bottom one.

- **Intersection**: When you perform an intersection of two paths, all that will remain is the area that was overlapping in both paths.

- **Exclusion**: When two paths are combined using the exclusion function, the resulting path keeps everything except the portions of the paths that were shared.

- **Division**: The first path as "drawn" will be split by the second and the outcome will be two or more paths.

♦ **Cut Path**: The first path is cut by the second drawn path, but the new paths have no fill, so the second path is a "cut out" of the first.

Time for action – creating an icon

We'll create an icon that has a border and star cut out. Let's get started:

1. Open a new document in Inkscape.

2. Select the create circles, ellipses, and arcs tool and draw a simple circle on the canvas. Hold the *Ctrl* key as you draw the circle to make it a perfect circle as follows:

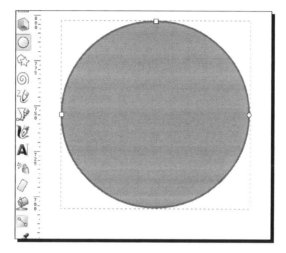

3. Use the **Fill and Stroke** dialog to remove the stroke and add an orange fill, as shown in the following image:

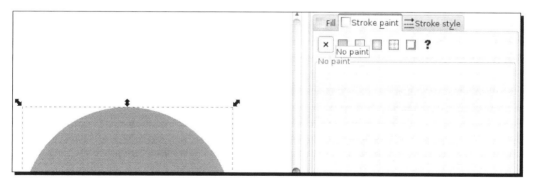

4. Select the star tool from the toolbox:

Make sure that you have the star option selected in the control bar as well:

5. Draw a star in the middle of the circle. This star can have any color fill and stroke, as shown in the following image:

6. Select the circle and the star. From the main menu, select **Object | Align and Distribute**.

In the **Align and Distribute** dialog, click center on the vertical axis and then click on the horizontal axis as follows:

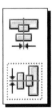

7. From the main menu, select **Path | Exclusion**.

You should then see that the circle has a "cut out" of a star in the middle as follows:

8. Select the create circles, ellipses, and arcs tool again and draw a simple circle just smaller than the first and overlap it on the circle/star icon. Make this circle have no fill, but a white stroke that is 1px in weight:

9. From the main menu, choose **File | Save** to save this project for future use.

What just happened?

We created a simple icon that used the exclusion feature for paths.

There is also an **Icon View** option in Inkscape. If you want to see how your project would look as an icon, select all objects on all layers (*Ctrl + Alt + A* keyboard shortcut), and from the menu, choose **View | Icon Preview**. Check the selection box. A preview of your icon is displayed in the most common size.

Summary

We learned a lot about paths in this chapter. We first just learned the basics about using them and the Bezier tool. Then we learned about transforming paths and how to convert shapes and strokes into paths so we could adjust them using nodes. We explored all path options, combining and breaking paths, as well as path placement and how it transforms shapes. Next up is styling text.

8

How to Style Text

The idea of text styling is to manipulate text so that it creates a certain feel when seen in an overall design. In the graphic design world, text styling is called typography and is a form of typesetting. Compare the look and feel (or design) of your local newspaper with that of children's magazines or start comparing web designs of the same—a newspaper site or a children's television network and compare it to a sports website. As seen, text is an important element in design.

Let's use this chapter to learn more about how we can manipulate and style text for any design. Here's what we will cover:

- ◆ Text and font editor
- ◆ Using paths and text
- ◆ Text and frames
- ◆ Spell check and find/replace
- ◆ Text effects
- ◆ Using text reflections

Text and Font editor

The **Text and Font editor** allows you to create text on your canvas and format it with the right font, size, and even kern. Let's open the editor and get started.

Time for action – opening and using the Text and Font editor

Creating text in a project is simple—select the **Create and Edit Text** tool in the toolbox, click at the insertion point within an open project, and start typing.

The text is immediately displayed on the canvas.

 The text tool (**A** icon) in the toolbox is the only way of creating new text on the canvas. The **T** icon shown in the command bar is used only when editing text that already exists on the canvas.

Then you can use the **Text and Font** menu to change everything from the font, style, size, and justification. To open this window, from the main menu, select **Text** and then **Text and Font** (or use the shortcut keys and press *Shift+Ctrl+T,* or the **T** icon in the command bar).

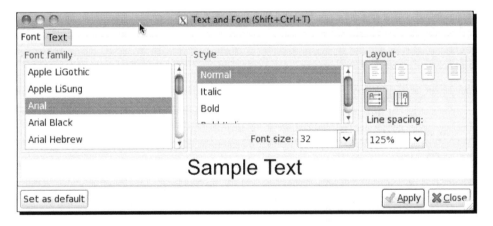

This window dialog also has a useful feature where you can edit your text directly. Click the **Text** tab and select the text you want to change or add/delete.

Back in the **Font** tab, you can change the font itself, the point size, alignment, line spacing, and even change from a horizontal to vertical text layout. But note, even though there are options for **Bold**, **Italics**, and **Bold Italics**, there is no option for underline. You can, however, use the **Bezier** or line tool to give you the same effect as the underline feature.

> **Spacing shortcut keys**
>
> You can also change the spacing of selected text by using shortcut keys. Use the *Alt + >* or *Alt + <* keys to try it out. For more information about keyboard shortcuts, see *Appendix A, Keyboard Shortcuts*.

What just happened?

You opened the **Text and Font** editor and added some text to your canvas. We also saw how you can change the font, point size, alignment, line spacing, and even how to adjust horizontal and vertical text layout.

Pop quiz – font options

1. What font options do you have available in Inkscape?

    a. Bold

    b. Bold Italics

    c. Underline

    d. Italics

    e. A, B, and D

Kerning

One of the more important items in typography and working with text that you will want to learn about is **kerning**—or the ability to adjust the spacing between letters.

There is no menu path to perform this in Inkscape. Instead, you can use handy shortcut keys. For more information about keyboard shortcuts, see *Appendix A, Keyboard Shortcuts*.

Time for action – kerning text

Here's how to kern text that already exists on your canvas:

1. First, double-click some text you have already entered in an open project. This will take you into the **Create and Edit Text** tool, allowing you to edit the text letter-by-letter.

2. Using the arrow keys, move the cursor between the two letters you want to add or diminish space between.

3. Then, press the *Alt* + right arrow key to add space between the letters. Alternatively, press the *Alt* + left arrow key to lessen the space between those two letters. Keep an eye on the kerning value in the Tool control bar **A | A**. It is set in pixels and displays fractions of the value of space between the letters.

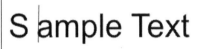

4. Alternatively, if you want to move individual (or multiple) characters up and down—just move your cursor near the letter (or letters) you want to move vertically.

5. Select the letter(s) by using the *Shift* key and the right/left arrows or drag your mouse over the character(s) you want to edit.

6. Then press *Alt* + up key to move the letter(s) up from the horizontal baseline. Again, see the Tools control bar setting A|A for the specific spacing.

7. Alternatively, you can use the *Alt* + down key combination to move a letter down from the horizontal baseline.

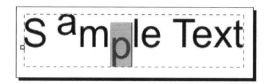

8. You can even rotate letters. Select a letter you want to rotate left or right and then use the *Alt* + *[* or *]* key to start moving it. The Tools control bar can, again, help you with exact spacing information.

9. Feel free to save the file now if you think you might want to use this going forward.

 Baseline shift and letter rotation functions are only available to text that is *not* inside a flowed text frame.

What just happened?

You created some text on your canvas and then adjusted the kerning (or spacing) of letters. We even rotated and dropped lettings below (and above) the horizontal baseline for a different sort of text styling technique.

When adjusting kerning in Inkscape, it is convenient to leave the letters as text—instead of the alternative of converting the text to paths—as the text remains editable. You can easily switch fonts, change font sizes and styles, all without removing the kerning and spacing information that you have already set. One small disadvantage to this approach is that when you reopen (or deliver) an SVG file, you must have the original font used in this file's creation on the computer. Just remember when providing and saving the SVG file to keep all graphics and fonts used in the creation of the web design or graphic together and available for any future use.

 You can also create a duplicate layer (**File | Layer | Duplicate**) and then hide it to preserve text styling for future rework of the document and text information.

Text styling keyboard shortcuts

Since not all text styling options are available via a menu item, here's an overview of most text options available via keyboard shortcuts. Also refer to *Appendix A, Keyboard Shortcuts* for all key combination shortcuts available for Inkscape.

Text Selection Shortcut Keys	
Ctrl + left/right arrows	Cursor moves word-by-word
Shift + left/right arrows	Selects/deselects letter-by-letter
Ctrl + *Shift* + left/right arrows	Selects/deselects word-by-word
Double-click on letters	Selects the word
Triple-click	Selects the entire line of text
Shift + *Home* For Mac OS: *Shift* + *Fn* + left arrow	Selects from the beginning of the line up to the cursor position
Shift + *End* For Mac OS: *Shift* + *Fn* + right arrow	Selects from the cursor to the end of the line
Ctrl + *Shift* + *Home* For Mac OS: *Ctrl* + Shift + *Fn* + left arrow	Selects from the beginning of the text up to the cursor position
Ctrl + *Shift* + *End* For Mac OS: *Ctrl* + *Shift* + *Fn* + right arrow	Selects from the cursor position up to the end of the text

Hot Keys	
Ctrl + B	Applies bold style to the selected text
Ctrl + I	Applies italic style to the selected text
Alt + right or left arrows	Increase or decrease the space between characters (kerning)
Alt + > or < keys	Changes the overall letter spacing within a text box
Alt + [or] keys	Rotates letters
Alt + up or down arrows	Changes the vertical position of the selected text, relative to the baseline
Alt + *Shift* + arrows	Moves position by 10 pixel steps
Ctrl + [or]	Rotates 90°

Using paths and text

Using paths with text is a great combination to make unique designs for banners, logos, and headings or footers, on various business documents. They work together and allow you to have complete control over how the text will look. Let's review how we can make them work together.

Time for action – using a path for text

In Inkscape, you can put text onto a path and have it follow its shape—and when you do this, the text and the path remain editable, which means you can still change the text, the shape of the path, kerning, and spacing elements in the text. Let's look at an example:

1. To start, draw a path with the **Bezier** tool or in the case of the following example, the spiral tool.

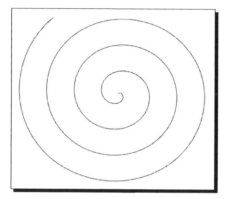

2. Then use the text tool and type the text that you would like to place on the path.

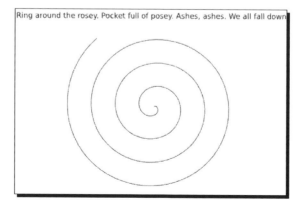

3. Select both the text and path.

4. Then, from the main menu, select **Text** and then **Put on Path**. You'll see that the text then is literally placed on the path of the line you had drawn.

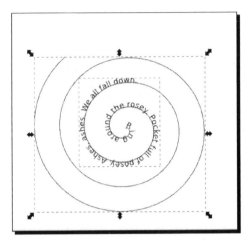

5. You can now move the original path and the text moves along with it. Alternatively, you can move the text away from the path, edit the text, or transform the text using kerning, text size, rotating letters, or moving them from the baseline—but it will still hold the shape of the path.

6. If you need to remove the shape from the text, from the main menu, select **Text** and then **Remove from Path**. You'll see that the text will turn back to a regular text object.

7. If you want the text to maintain the shape of the path, but hide the actual shape, select the path and change its opacity to 0, in essence, hiding the path.

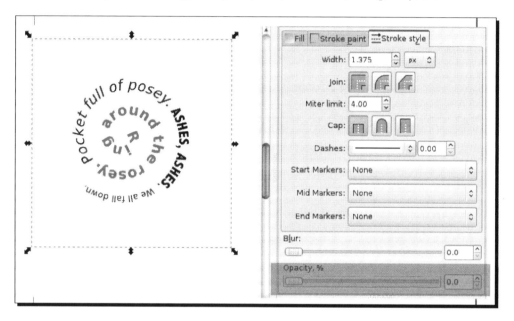

What just happened?

You placed some text on a path of an object or shape. You also learned how to manipulate the text while it is placed on the page, as well as how to remove the text from the shape and hide the path itself so that you keep the text shape.

Placing text within a closed shape

Another unique form of text styling can be done by placing text within a shape. Words will automatically wrap so that the text fits as best as possible within the shape. You can, of course, still edit the text after this, and even change some of its features.

Time for action – placing text in a closed shape

Let's walk through an example of how to place the words "Twinkle, twinkle little star" into a star object:

1. First create a star in a new Inkscape document.

2. Select the **Create and Edit Text** tool from the toolbox and type the text onto the canvas.

> Twinkle, twinkle little star. How I wonder what you are. Up above the world so high, like a diamond in the sky. Twinkle, twinkle, little star.

3. Select both the text and the star. Then from the main menu, choose **Text** and then **Flow into Frame**. Instantly, you'll see that the text is placed, as best as it can be, within the confines of the shape.

> Twinkle, twinkle little star. How I wonder what you are. Up above the world so high, like a diamond in the sky. Twinkle, twinkle, little star.

4. Feel free to manipulate the text to make it look just right, even changing color, kerning, and spacing if needed. Similarly you can change the color, stroke, and position of the shape to see how the text reacts as well as the impact on the overall design.

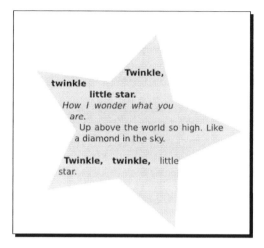

5. If you ever want to remove the text from the shape, from the main menu, choose **Text** and then **Unflow**.

6. Save the file in the Inkscape SVG format if you plan to use this file in any future projects!

What just happened?

We took some simple text and then placed it within a shape. Then we took that text and manipulated it so that it would take the *shape* of another object. Lastly, we rotated and manipulated the container shape to have the best impact on the design.

Spell check and find/replace

Just like in a word processing program, you can find and replace a word (or term) in the text box of an Inkscape document.

Time for action – performing a find and replace

We will perform a simple find and replace in the following example. To do this:

1. In an open project, choose the **Create and Edit Text** tool and select an already-created text box with content residing in it.

2. From the main menu, select **Extensions** and then **Text** and **Replace Text**.

3. In the **Replace text** dialog box, place the word you want to replace in the first field and the new word in the second field.

4. Click **Apply** and every instance of the old word will be replaced within the selected text box.

Remember, using this process will replace every single instance of a word in the selected text. If you only want to replace certain instances of the word, this process might be superseded by some careful proofreading of the content.

What just happened?

We found the menu options in order to perform a search and replace for words within a text frame in Inkscape.

Text effects

Inkscape gives a variety of options for manipulating text within its extensions. Let's go through a few examples.

Time for action – using text effects

We will perform a number of text effects that are available in Inkscape. Let's get started:

1. **Sentence case**: This simply means using capital letters as you would in sentences—it replaces lowercase characters with capitals at the beginning of every sentence.

    The quick brown fox jumps over the lazy dog.

    To use this in Inkscape:

    ❑ In an open project, choose the **Create and Edit Text** tool and select an already-created text box with content residing in it.

    ❑ From the main menu, select **Extensions** and then **Text** and **Sentence Case**. All capitalization rules will change to sentence case.

2. **Title case**: Instead of capitalizing the first word in every sentence like the previous example, this text effect capitalizes the first letter of every word in the text box.

    ❑ In an open project, choose the **Create and Edit Text** tool and select an already-created text box with content residing in it.

    ❑ From the main menu, select **Extensions**, **Text**, and **Title Case**. All capitalization rules will change to be title case.

    The Quick Brown Fox Jumps Over The Lazy Dog.

3. **Uppercase and lowercase**: These effects simply change the case of each letter in the text box. The uppercase effect makes each letter a capital, whereas the lowercase effect changes all letters to their lowercase form.

    THE QUICK BROWN FOX JUMPS OVER THE LAZY DOG.
    the quick brown fox jumps over the lazy dog.

    As with the other effects you do this as follows:

    ❑ In an open project, choose the text tool and select an already-created text box with content residing in it.

    ❑ From the main menu, select **Extensions, Text** and then **Uppercase** or **Lowercase**. All capitalization rules will change as specified.

4. **Flipcase**: This is a fun effect for text. It reverses the written letter case, so all capitals will become lowercase, and all lowercase letters become uppercase letters. It looks like this:

> The Quick Brown Fox Jumps Over The Lazy Dog.
>
> tHE qUICK bROWN fOX jUMPS oVER tHE lAZY dOG.

Again, this is accessed from the Effect menu:

- ❏ In an open project, choose the text tool and select an already-created text box with content residing in it.
- ❏ From the main menu, select **Extensions** and then **Text** and **fLIP cASE**.

5. **Random case**: This is also a fun text effect; it takes the text contained in a text box and arbitrarily toggles the letter case throughout. To use it:

- ❏ In an open project, choose the text tool and select an already-created text box with content residing in it.
- ❏ From the main menu, select **Extensions** and then **Text** and **rANdOm CasE**. The result looks something like this:

> tHe qUICk bRoWn FoX JUMps oVEr tHe lAZy DOg.

What just happened?

We learned the basics of creating text and manipulating it in Inkscape with extensions. Specifically, we dived into text effects, learning the differences between title case, sentence case, upper and lowercase, flip case, and random case in Inkscape. We even worked on examples of each type for reference.

Creating text reflections

One common effect seen with text elements is creating a reflection or shadow of the letters in the word. This effect gives the words more presence without much additional work (and doesn't overdo the text). We'll learn how to do both with some example text.

Time for action – creating a reflection

In this example, we're aiming to create a simple text heading that has a reflection below it and then to add a little something special (but very simple) to the text to make it stand apart with very few additional effects. Here's what we'll create:

1. Open a new document in Inkscape, create a text box, and enter some text. In our example, we'll use the word: **REFLECTIONS**.

2. Next, we are going to clone the image. From the main menu, select **Edit**, **Clone**, and then **Create Clone**.

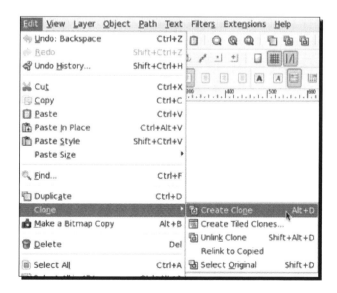

3. Now we need to flip the cloned image vertically to create the basics for our reflection. An easy way to do this is to press the *V* key (or from the main menu, select **Object** and then **Flip Vertically**).

4. Move the *flipped* image below the original text.

5. From the toolbox, select the rectangle tool and create a rectangle that covers the reflected (or cloned) image.

6. Now we need to set a gradient on this rectangle. To start, make sure to set the fill to black.

7. Click the gradient tool near the bottom of the toolbox.

8. Click near the middle of the rectangle and drag upward to set gradient (from dark on the bottom to light on the top).

9. By default the Inkscape gradient applies an alpha setting of 0 to the stop gradient, which will be fully transparent. This means, in the preceding image, the top side of the rectangle and the gradient would be transparent. Click **Edit** in the control bar to change this setting.

10. Choose the transparent stop to edit.

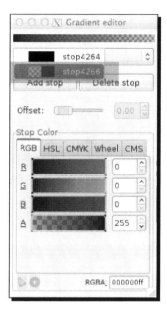

11. Now change the **R**, **G**, and **B** values to `255`, so that it is white.

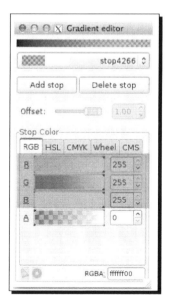

12. Select both the rectangle and the reflected text behind. Use the select tool, and drag a bounding box around the rectangle. You should see a dotted line around the rectangle and the text behind it. Alternatively, you can select the text below by using *Alt* and clicking the text's approximate location and then pressing *Shift* and clicking on the rectangle.

13. From the main menu, select **Object**, then **Mask**, and then **Set**. Essentially you are **masking** the reflection (cloned) text with the gradient box. Thus the reflection text takes on the levels of gray of the object in front of it. That is why it looks very much like a reflection.

14. If the reflection still seems a bit dark for your taste, change the opacity from the **Fill and Stroke** dialog box.

15. But let's spice up this text just a little bit more. Select the first letter and let's change the color and also increase the point size of that letter by at least 8 points—voila! Since you cloned the image, any change you make to original text will also be changed in the reflection automatically.

16. Feel free to save this file for future reference or to use in your current projects.

What just happened?

We created a reflection of text in Inkscape. We did this by creating text, using a clone, and then using a mask in order to create the actual reflection text. There are a number of other ways to create a reflection—that involve just creating a gradient on the cloned/flipped text itself. However, the process described in the preceding section allows you to still edit the text directly and the reflection will update as well.

Pop Quiz – transparency

1. In Inkscape, by default, the Alpha setting or Stop of gradients is white.

    a. True

    b. False

Summary

You've learned a lot about text editing and styling in this chapter. Specifically, there were details about the text editor, methods of using and manipulating text such as kerning, rotating, and moving letters from the baseline. You even learned how to have text follow a path and create text frames for larger blocks of text and finally create a reflection with the text. We will expand upon what we have learned and do more of this in the next chapter, *Using Filters*.

9
Using Filters

This chapter will focus on using filters with text and images to give a further dimension to your vector graphics. We will start by explaining what filters are, how to find them in Inkscape, and then dive into specific filter examples with both images and texttext, including a detailed example of step-by-step instructions on using filters with text.

Here are the details of what we will discuss in the chapter:

◆ What are filters?
◆ Using the filter editor
◆ Using filters with text
◆ Images and effects

What are filters?

In Inkscape, think of a filter as something superimposed on top of a vector object giving it features that are much like a raster-based image. Examples of filters or filter effects are blurring, shadows, and glows. These effects are only an overlay—so can be turned on/off at any time and modified whenever needed, in essence, giving the vector-object properties most commonly seen on other graphic types.

Using the Filter editor

To view all the filters that Inkscape has to offer (there are hundreds of them installed by default), on the main menu, select **Filters**:

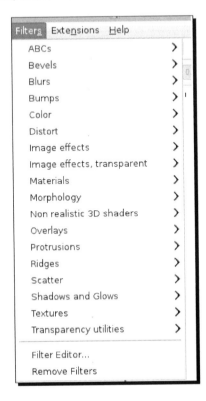

There are two categories of filters: the ones that work with normal objects (such as a created vector object in Inkscape) and the others that work with bitmaps (such as images or PNG files you have imported into Inkscape). Watch the notification area along the bottom of the screen when you use the filter menu for which filters will work on your selected objects as follows:

Since there are many filters to use with Inkscape, it may seem overwhelming to know which one to use. You should explore and test to see which ones work best for your design or drawing.

Let's work through an example about how to use one of the filters in Inkscape.

Time for action – using filters

In this example, let's create an icon, such as the example shown as follows:

Let's give it a drop shadow, which is one of the more common filter effects used in Inkscape and almost all image editing software as it is an essential filter for creating a sense of realism:

1. Open a new Inkscape document.

2. From the main menu, select **File**, **New**, and then **icon_64x64**.

 Icon sizes can vary depending on your design (or what operating system you might be creating them for), so feel free to change your canvas sizes accordingly.

3. From the main menu, select **View** and then **Grid**. Having the grid viewable will help us with the spacing of all the objects.

4. Let's again set the grid properties. From the main menu, select **File** and then **Document Properties**.

5. Select the **Grid** tab and verify that **Spacing X** and **Spacing Y** are both set to **1.0** and that **Major Grid Lines** is set to every 4 pixels.

6. Close the **Document Properties** dialog by clicking the red X in the upper-left corner.

7. Make sure the snap bounding box corners icon is selected.

8. Let's start by creating the main part of the icon. Use the rectangle tool to draw a rectangle in the center of the canvas (there will be one box grid around the rectangle) as follows:

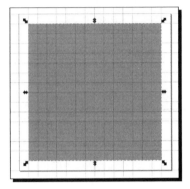

9. Double-click the square, so the handles change to corner nodes:

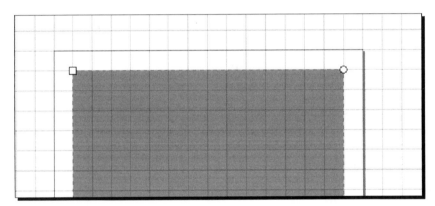

10. Drag the upper-right circle handle inward. You will see that the corners of the rectangle now become rounded, as shown in the following image:

11. Use the **Fill and Stroke** dialog to give the rectangle a bright fill color. This will keep the edges of the icon clean and crisp.

12. Next we'll add our first filter. Select the rectangle object and select **Filter | Blur | Evanescent**:

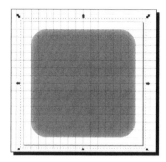

13. Select the star tool and draw one within the rectangle, as shown in the following image:

14. Select all of the icon elements using the keyboard shortcut *Ctrl + A*, then use the keyboard shortcut *Shift + Ctrl + A* to open the **Alignment** menu. Choose the **Page** in the **Relative to:** drop-down menu and then click the center of the vertical axis icon.

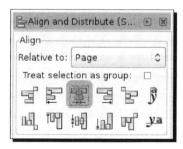

15. Now let's give the star a drop shadow. Select the star and then from the main menu, select **Filters**, **Shadows and Glows**, and then **Drop Shadow**. Use settings similar to that shown in the following screenshot:

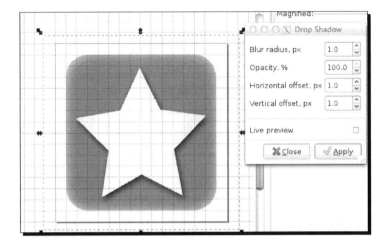

16. Let's give our overall rectangle object a drop shadow as well. Keeping the **Drop Shadow** window displayed, select the rectangle.

17. Click **Apply** in the **Drop Shadow** window (to keep the same **Drop Shadow** settings as the star):

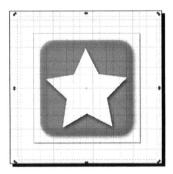

18. Save your file using a nomenclature that represents a collection of icons that you can create with these same document properties, color characteristics, and similar styles for future project use.

What just happened?

We created a simple icon, used an image filter, and the drop shadow filter effect—a complex filter – to give the icon some depth.

To preview this as an icon, select all objects on all layers (*Ctrl + Alt + A* is the keyboard shortcut), and from the menu, choose **View | Icon Preview**. Check the selection box. A preview of your icon is displayed in the most common size.

Pop quiz – common icon sizes

1. What icon size below is NOT found in the icon preview option in Inkscape?

    a. 16 x 16

    b. 40 x 40

    c. 48 x 48

    d. 32 x 32

    e. 24 x 24

    f. 128 x 128

Using filters with text

We created a reflection in Chapter 8 that used filters in Inkscape and you can use the same principles for creating text shadows as well. Let's work through an example and see whether other filters work well with text.

Time for action – using filters with text

We will create one example of how we can use filters with text to create a mood or feeling with text in design:

1. Open a new document in Inkscape, create a text box, and enter some text. In our example, we'll use the word: **BOO!**.

2. With the text selected, from the main menu, select **Filters**, **Textures**, and then choose **Ink Paint**:

There are a lot more filters here that you can use that will give neat effects for your text. These include Cutout, Cutout & Glow, Dark & Glow, Drop Glow, Fuzzy Glow, Glow, In and Out, Inner Glow, Inner Shadow, and Inset. See the following graphic for what each of these filters looks like when applied to our text examples. You can find these specific text filters on the main menu under **Filters | Shadows and Glows**:

 The effects strongly depend on the objects and their colors in the background. The examples were only rendered without objects in the background and thus some of the filters may require some tweaking in the **Filter** editor for a more refined look.

What just happened?

We added a simple **Ink Paint** filter to a set of words to add to the visual feeling we wanted to achieve in a design. Then we learned about other filters that might work well with text.

Images and effects

Inkscape doesn't allow for extensive photo manipulation. However, here are some basic effects to use with photographic images:

- ◆ Blurs
- ◆ Bumps
- ◆ Color
- ◆ Distort
- ◆ Image Effects

◆ Image Effects, Transparent

◆ Transparency Utilities

◆ Overlay filters

◆ For some fun, try Scatter and Texture filters and Clip with photographs as well.

Let's walk through using one of these filters as an example.

Time for action – using filters with images

Let's work with a photograph of a couple and see if we can enchance it for use on a cooking website:

1. Open a new Inkscape document and import a bitmap image. From the main menu, select **File** and then **Import**.

2. Select the correct bitmap file and click **Open**. Make sure your imported bitmap file is selected and then select **File** and then **Document Properties**. In the **Custom Size** section, click **Resize page to content**.

3. Click **Resize page to drawing or selection**.

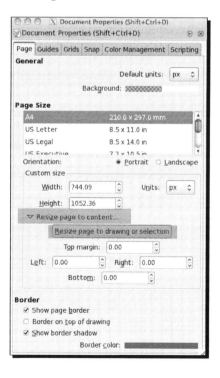

Your document page size will now be adjusted to match that of your imported bitmap image, as shown in the following screenshot:

4. Select the image and then from the main menu, select **Filters** and then **Image Effects** and **Soft Focus Lens**. This will create a "soft" image and give a dreamy effect as follows:

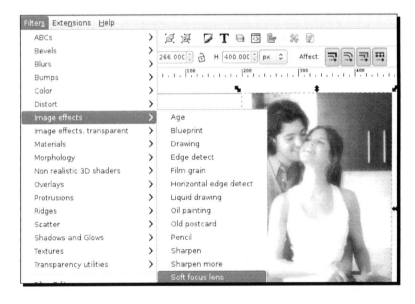

5. Next, we will create a "torn edge" effect around the photo by making sure the photo is selected and then from the main menu, choosing **Filters** and then **Distort** and **Torn edges** as follows:

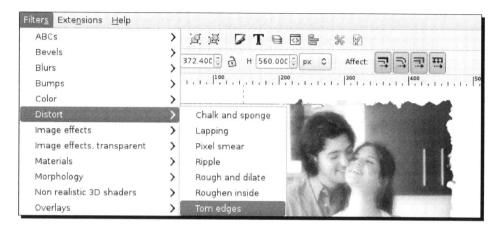

6. Now the photo can be saved as a PNG and placed in an overall design. To save this file, from the main menu, select **File** and then **Export**. Give it a filename and save it within the project file folders.

What just happened?

We imported a bitmap image (a photograph) and then added two filters to it—a blur and distortion filter of torn edges.

Tracing images

Tracing essentially creates the paths (and nodes) it identifies within a bitmap image and then uses those paths to create a vector-based image from the bitmap. Rendering in Inkscape is always done using **Potrace**, but there is an extra option called **Simple Interactive Object Extraction** (**SIOX**) that allows separation of an object from the background bitmap image.

The results of this tracing process depend heavily on the quality of the original images. Potrace works best for black-and-white line drawings or black-and-white pictures with high contrast. It can be used for screened color prints and color photography as well, but it can require a bit more careful detail and work to make it happen. Let's go through a couple of examples.

Time for action – using Potrace

We will start by importing another photograph bitmap image and then using Potrace:

1. Open up the bitmap image you want to trace in Inkscape. You can drag-and-drop an image onto the Inkscape window to import it.

2. Make sure the image is selected and then from the main menu, choose **Path** and then **Trace Bitmap**. The **Trace Bitmap** dialog box appears.

3. The **Mode** tab defines characteristics of the tracing mode as follows:

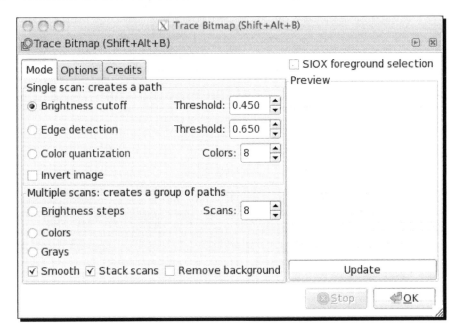

For this picture, we will set the following:

- **Single scan**
- **Brightness cutoff: Threshold 0.450**

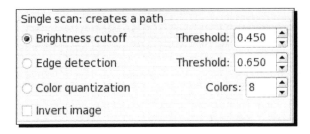

4. Click the **Options** tab to set some additional options as follows:

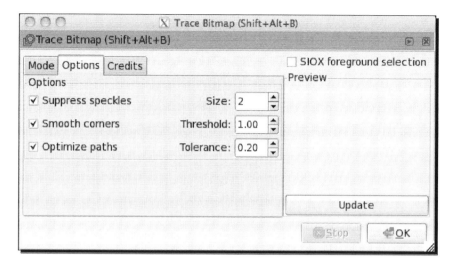

These options are used across either the single or multiple scan mode.

For this sample, we'll select the checkboxes for all options (essentially turning them on) with these settings:

- **Suppress speckles: Size 2**
- **Smooth corners: Threshold 1.00**
- **Optimize paths: Tolerance 0.20**

5. When all settings are in place, click **OK** to perform the conversion.

6. Within a few moments, you will be able to see the results.

You'll notice your original image will still be viewable on the canvas. Click to select the traced paths and then drag it off of the original image (which is underneath). Alternatively, from the main menu, select **Object** and then **Lower**—to lower the new image below the original:

7. Select the original image and hide it in the **Layers** dialog. Your new vector image should be viewable.

8. Save this new file (choose **File** and then **Save As...**) with a new descriptive filename and be sure that the file type in the bottom-right is **Inkscape SVG**:

What just happened?

In this example, we kept the background in place and created a vector image from a photograph.

However, another scenario is that you want to take one object from the picture and create a vector object from that one object. That is where using the option **SIOX** comes into play. Let's learn how to use it in the next section.

Time for action – using SIOX

SIOX means **Simple Interactive Object Extraction**. It lets you separate an object from the background in a bitmap image. If you paid close attention to the steps performed to do a trace in the previous section, you'll notice that the option to use this feature is within the **Tracing Bitmap** dialog box.

Using SIOX depends on the characteristics of the bitmap image. If you have a photograph where an object is clearly distinguished in color from the background—you have a great chance for success in recreating it with a trace using this feature. Here's how it's done:

1. Open up the bitmap image you want to trace in Inkscape.

2. Make sure the image is selected and then from the main menu, choose **Path** and then **Trace Bitmap**. The **Trace Bitmap** dialog box appears.

3. Check the **SIOX foreground selection** box to turn it on, as shown in the following screenshot:

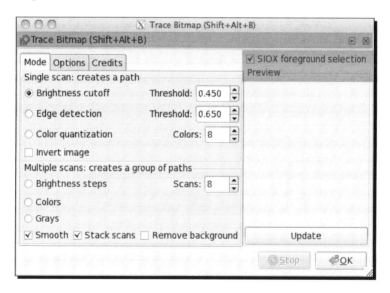

4. Now, use the freehand tool or a box, circle, or another object, and select an area of the image that includes the entire object you want to extract, and some of the background, as follows:

5. Give the path an opaque fill if it doesn't already have one.

6. Select both the bitmap image and the path and then perform a trace by clicking **OK** in the **Trace Bitmap** dialog box:

7. Within a few moments, you'll see the background disappear from the canvas. Select the opaque object used in the process and delete it to show your final image:

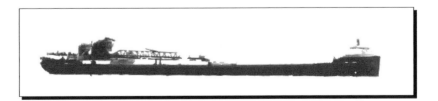

8. Save your new image in SVG format – it's now a vector graphic!

 In the example, we used a rectangle object to select the main point of interest and some of the background. However, you can use the freehand Bezier tool as well to draw around irregular objects and do the same process.

What just happened?

We took a full photograph image and then essentially pulled an object from that photograph and made it a vector graphic via the tracing effect.

Ultimately, tracing bitmap images so that they can be turned into vector graphics takes some practice and trial-and-error. However, if you can do this well, you will use it in a variety of projects—anywhere from web design to helping to create and clean up logos and more.

Summary

We spent this entire chapter discussing filters and filter effects, learning where they are used in Inkscape, and then how to create a filter effect for a vector object.

The last half of the chapter was dedicated to examples of using Potrace and SIOX. The next chapter will be dedicated to extensions in Inkscape.

10

Extensions in Inkscape

In Inkscape there are a number of extensions—templates and plugins that can assist in the design process for vector graphics. At the very least, they decrease preparation time when starting a new mockup.

This chapter will discuss templates in detail, and then plugins and scripts. Specifically:

- ◆ What templates are
- ◆ Installing and using new templates
- ◆ What extensions are
- ◆ Available extensions and scripts
- ◆ Installing and using extensions

Templates

Inkscape has some pre-defined templates you can use to start your development.
To access these templates, go to the main menu and select **File** and then **New**. A pop-up menu appears showing a number of default page (or canvas) sizes to choose from, as shown in the following screenshot:

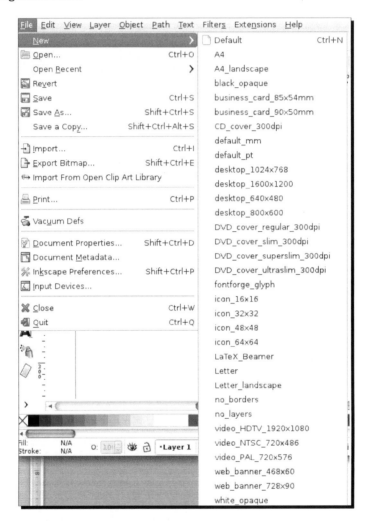

Installing and using new templates

Most templates are pre-loaded into the Inkscape release and installation. However, if you find additional Inkscape templates you want to use, they can be easily installed.

Time for action – installing Inkscape templates

To install a template in Inkscape, do the following:

1. Download the new template file. If it is in a compressed format (ZIP, RAR, and so on), uncompress or extract the SVG template file. You can use applications such as WinZip, WinRAR, or 7-Zip to extract files such as these.

2. Open the SVG file itself in Inkscape to view the template to make sure it fits your needs.

3. From the main menu, select **File** and then **Save As**. Choose a save location in your computer operating system's Inkscape template directory:

  - For Windows, that directory is the `C:\Program Files\Inkscape\share\templates` folder

  - For Mac OS, the directory is `/Applications/Inkscape/Contents/Resources/Templates/`

  - For Linux, the directory is typically `/usr/local/share/inkscape/templates` or `/home/user/.config/inkscape/templates`

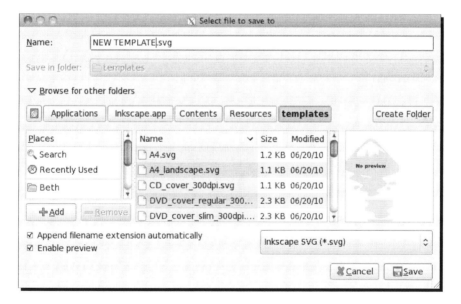

4. Click **Save**.

5. If you restart Inkscape and go to the main menu and select **File** and then **New**, the new custom template should be in the submenu.

What just happened?

With a few simple steps, you downloaded new templates for Inkscape, uncompressed those files, and saved them to your hard drive. Then, after restarting Inkscape, the new templates were installed and available for use.

Creating your own custom templates

If you need to create your own template, or modify one of these existing options, there are a few ways you can then save it for use in future projects. Let's see how to start a custom template.

Time for action – modifying an existing Inkscape template

To modify an existing template:

1. Open the template that most resembles the new one you would like to create.

2. Modify the **Document Properties** (choose **File** and then **Document Properties** or use the *Shift + Ctrl/Option + D* keyboard shortcut) or other settings applicable to the template you want to create, as shown in the following screenshot:

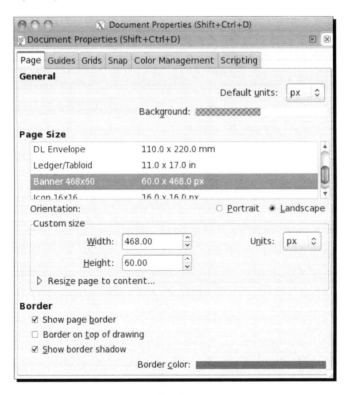

3. From the main menu, choose **File** and then **Save As**, choosing to save the file to your computer operating system's Inkscape template directory.

4. Once saved, restart Inkscape and go to the main menu. Select **File** and then **New**—and the new custom template should be in the submenu.

What just happened?

We modified an existing template in Inkscape to use as a base for others. We then saved the template so we can use it for other projects.

Time for action – creating a custom template

If you want to create a new template from scratch, this is almost as easy:

1. Open a new Inkscape file.

2. From the main menu, choose **File** and then **Document Properties** or use the *Shift + Ctrl/Option + D* keyboard shortcut.

3. Adjust all settings applicable to the template you want to create and save the file to your computer operating system's Inkscape template directory.

4. Once saved, restart Inkscape and go to the main menu. Select **File** and then **New**—and the new custom template should be in the submenu.

What just happened?

A template file of any kind (used from default, created for your use only, or modified templates) contains the document settings and normally does not contain SVG objects. When saved in the template folder, you can select the template from the drop-down menu for new documents.

In the previous steps, we created a custom template for Inkscape.

What are extensions?

Let's first understand what extensions are in Inkscape. **Extensions** add new capabilities to software programs—thus customizing what you want them to do for you.

When you use **scripts** with Inkscape, you essentially add new features to the existing software. A script takes control of the Inkscape software to perform a certain feature. Scripts themselves differ from extensions in that they are usually written in a different programming language from the main program (Inkscape in this case) and can be modified at any time—mostly by Inkscape developers.

Extensions "extend" Inkscape's features or functionality .If you used an extension outside of inkscape, it wouldn't work correctly. An example of an extension for Inkscape is one that allows importing and exporting of non-SVG file types into the program. Most extensions require external programs, usually written in Perl or Python.

You can find common extensions here: `http://wiki.inkscape.org/wiki/index.php/ExtensionsRepository#Extensions`. Although they are not all-inclusive lists of what is available, they give you a healthy start in your search for customizing Inkscape.

Inkscape also comes with some pre-installed extensions. You find these in the main menu. Click **Extensions** and the submenu appears as follows:

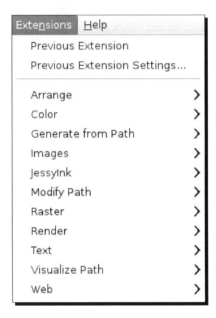

Examples of extension tutorials

There are many valuable extensions in Inkscape such as interpolate, scatter, and render. Here's a quick look at some tutorials online that can help you understand some of these extensions:

- Inkscape tutorial: Interpolate

  `http://inkscape.org/doc/interpolate/tutorial-interpolate.en.html`

- Inkscape 'Pattern along Path and 'Scatter' scripts:

  `http://math.univ-lille1.fr/~barraud/Inkscape/pathdeform/`

◆ Inkscape: Generate from path

   ```
   http://tavmjong.free.fr/INKSCAPE/MANUAL/html/Extensions-
   GenerateFromPath.html
   ```

◆ Inkscape tutorial: Fancy Borders

   ```
   http://verysimpledesigns.com/vectors/inkscape-tutorial-fancy-
   borders.html
   ```

Installation extensions

The procedures for installing plugins vary because there are some dependencies on your computer's operating system and on what software you already have installed on your computer. The best rule of thumb is to read the plugin installation instructions.

Script installation is a bit easier—it requires the script code file itself and an INX file. It is as simple as copying both files and placing them into the extension folder directly. In Windows, this directory is `C:\Program Files\Inkscape\share\extensions`. In the Mac OS and Linux, this is typically in the `home/.inkscape/extensions` directory.

You should always be sure to read script installation instructions because they often have dependencies. For example, they may require additional programs to be installed before they can work. If you don't know these dependencies up front, you can try an install and then read the error message after you run the script from a command-line interface.

Pop quiz – what are extensions?

True or false: Extensions add new capabilities to Inkscape and thus extend its features or functionality and on their own, outside of their use in Inkscape, wouldn't work correctly.

Summary

We dug right in at the start of this chapter and reviewed how to access the pre-installed templates in Inkscape. Then we took a look at how to install new templates that we might find online. We discussed in detail how to modify a standard template, save it as a custom one, and how to start from scratch and save a custom template. We also jumped into learning about extensions. Some sample tutorial links were also given to provide examples of how to use extensions in Inkscape as well as installing additional ones in Inkscape.

11
Working with Images

We talked a lot in the first chapter about rasterized versus vectorized images and how Inkscape is best used for vector graphics. But what if you only have rasterized images? Can you import them into Inkscape, manipulate them, or even save them as vector images? Of course you can. There are some minor limitations on how you export rasterized images, but this feature is often used to import the image and then manipulate it a bit for the vector use you need.

This chapter will focus on:

◆ Rendering a bitmap image

◆ Working with photographs and filters

Importing from the Open Clip Art Library (Linux and Mac users)

The Open Clip Art Library is an open source, free clip art image library that you can search directly from Inkscape.

 Unfortunately, the Open Clip Art Library menu options do not exist for Windows users. However, you can always go to www.openclipart.org in a web browser to view all available clip art, download, and then import into your projects.

This clip art library is searchable and most of its graphics can be used in your designs as needed (and as seen throughout this book). Let's see how we can use it.

Time for action – using the Open Clip Art Library (Mac users only)

Here's how it works:

1. In an open Inkscape project, from the main menu, choose **File** and then **Import From Open Clip Art Library**.

2. In the **Import From Open Clip Art Library** dialog box, in the **Search for:** field, enter a keyword to describe the clip art you want to place in the document and click **Search**, as shown in the following screenshot:

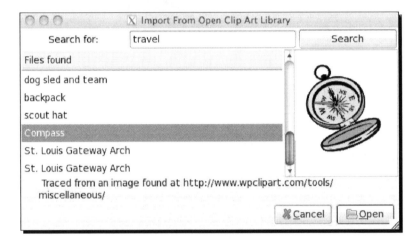

Inkscape then connects to the Open Clip Art Library website. Previews of files are shown in a window on the right-hand side of the dialog.

3. Try other keyword searches until you find one you like and then double-click the name of the image to place it in the document.

What just happened?

You opened the Open Clip Art Library via Inkscape, searched for a clip art image, and placed it on an Inkscape canvas.

The clip art library can be useful in a number of ways:

♦   It allows for free use of a number of images that you may like to use in a web design mockup, for placement or for end use.

♦   You can also ungroup the pieces of the image and adjust colors, remove items, edit the overall image, and use it in your own design:

Importing clip art images can give you a starting point for your own designs—as well as give great layout perspective when creating website mockups.

Pop quiz – Open Clip Art

1. Graphics downloaded from the Open Clip Art Library are:

    a. Free to use

    b. Editable (ungroup, adjust colors, remove items, edit the overall image)

    c. Downloadable in SVG format

    d. All of the above

Basics about photo manipulation

Inkscape doesn't allow for extensive photo manipulation, but these filters will work with photographs or non-vector based images. These are basic and fun effects for your photographic images. Filters that are photo (and bitmap) friendly are:

◆   Blurs

◆   Bumps

◆   Color

◆   Distort

◆   Image Effects

◆   Image Effects, Transparent

◆   Transparency Utilities

◆   Overlay

For some fun, try Scatter and Texture filters and Clip with photographs as well.

Let's walk through using one of these filters in a practical example.

Time for action – blurring the background of a photograph

We will take the same photograph we used from a previous exercise and manipulate it differently here. We will select the foreground that we want to keep crisp, and clear and then blur the background. Here are the steps on how this is done:

1. Open a new Inkscape document and import a bitmap/photograph you want to use for this exercise. From the main menu, select **File** and then **Import**.

2. Select the correct bitmap file and click **Open**. Make sure your imported bitmap is selected, and then select **File** and then **Document Properties**. In the **Custom Size** section, click **Resize page to content**, as shown in the following screenshot:

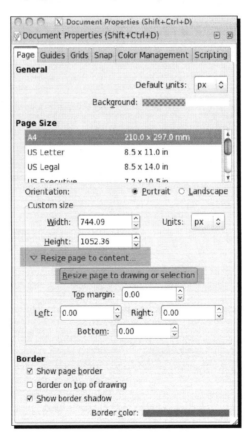

3. Click **Resize page to drawing or selection**.

Your document page size will now be adjusted to match that of your imported bitmap image, as shown in the following screenshot.

4. Select your photograph objects in the window and now choose **Edit** and **Duplicate** as follows:

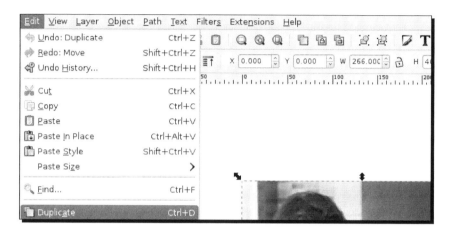

5. Select and then drag the top duplicate photograph off to the side of the canvas as follows:

Image credit Photostock at Freedigitalphotos.net

We will need to adjust that one later. It will be our "background" image.

6. Now we will need to create a clipping mask of the portion of the people we want to remain in the foreground of our picture. Select the **Bezier** tool and trace around the people's faces as follows:

7. You may need to zoom in to the photo to get a more detailed view to work with.

8. Note, when you use the **Bezier** tool, every time you click-and-drag, a new curve node is created.

9. You can also create rough shapes and then click between nodes to add new nodes and adjust as necessary. An example is shown as follows:

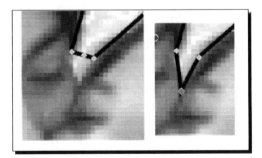

10. Once you "connect" the last node to the beginning one, it will "close" the tool and make a selection:

11. Now with the traced object and the original photo selected, from the main menu, select **Object | Clip | Set** as follows:

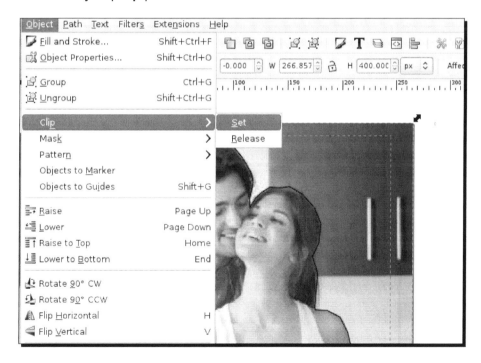

12. You will now see a clip of just the selected portions of the couple that you outlined previously:

13. Select and move the duplicate/background image back into place above the clipped image:

14. To make sure it all aligns properly, click the **Align and distribute objects** icon in the toolbar. The **Align and Distribute** dialog will appear on the right-hand side of your screen as follows:

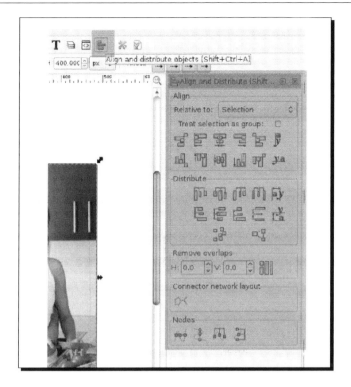

15. Make sure the **Relative to:** field is set to **Page** and click the align vertically and align horizontally icons as follows:

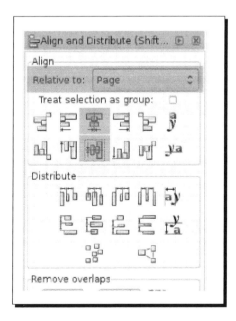

16. Click the X icon in the upper-right corner to close this dialog box.

17. Choose the **Fill and Stroke** icon on the toolbar. The **Fill and Stroke** dialog will now also appear on the right-hand side of the screen as follows:

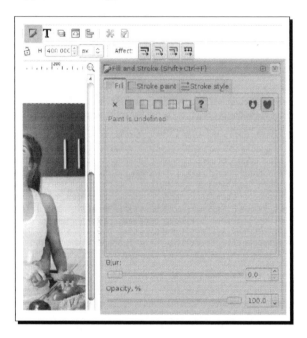

18. Make sure the full photograph duplicate is still selected on your canvas and move the **Blur** slider bar to the right until you like the blur amount:

19. Again, with the image still selected, choose the **Lower selection to bottom** icon in the top toolbar as follows:

20. You will see that this duplicate photograph will now drop behind the clipped image and we have a "blurred" background in our photograph!

21. Now the photo can be saved in a native Inkscape format for future editing or as a PNG file and placed in another design. To save this file, from the main menu, select **File** and then **Export**. Give it a filename and save it within the project file folders.

What just happened?

You took a standard photograph, brought it into Inkscape, and edited it so that the background was more blurred than the foreground.

We applied some non-destructive clipping and filtering to a photograph. That said, the image itself is untouched, and if you want to see the full effects of the background blurring, don't forget to export the image as a PNG file (**File | Export Bitmap**).

To edit the images directly, use the image extensions. Import the photograph and use the extensions found in the main menu option: **Extensions | Raster**.

Converting raster logos to vector-based logos

Many clients might only have their logo images in raster or bitmap formats—JPG, GIF, PNG, or BMP, which as we defined in *Chapter 1, Getting Started with Vector Graphics*, are a grid of pixels that are set to certain colors. When these logos are made larger, there's a loss of quality (remember the boxey, pixelated look?). Often, you might need to scale a logo larger so it fits in your new design and want to maintain smooth edges. You do this by converting it to a vector-based image.

Time for action – converting a logo to a vector-based image

Here's how you use Inkscape to convert a raster image logo into an SVG image in vector graphic format (that will be scalable!):

1. Open the logo you want to convert in Inkscape. Whenever possible use an image that is of as high resolution as possible. This will ensure the best possible recreation of the logo. You can see from the enlarged screenshot that the edges are not smooth, as shown in the following image:

2. Select the entire image (**Edit** and then **Select All**) and then perform a trace by choosing **Path** and then **Trace Bitmap**.

3. In the **Trace Bitmap** dialog box, select **Multiscan Colors** as the mode and be sure that **Smooth** is unchecked. The **Scans** can be set to **15**.

4. Click **OK** to start the conversion.

5. (Optional step) As needed, adjust the new vector conversion of the image. Add, move, and adjust the nodes to match the original raster more closely.

6. Next you need to delete your original image. From the main menu, select **Object** and then **Lower**—you will now see that your new vector image was "lowered" beneath the original jagged-edged image.

7. Select the original image and then press the *Delete* key on your keyboard. Your new vector image should be viewable as follows:

8. Tracing the image may not be enough to fully recreate the logo. Further clean-up and coloring of the image may still be required to obtain a high-quality logo.

9. Save this new file (choose **File** and then **Save As...**) with a new descriptive filename and be sure that the file type in the bottom-right is Inkscape SVG.

What just happened?

You took a logo file in JPG format and converted it into an Inkscape vector image that can be scaled larger (or smaller) and used like all vector graphics.

Summary

In this chapter, we learned a lot about working with images—raster and vector—in Inkscape. We looked at importing bitmap images, embedding images, rendering bitmap images, working a bit with photographs and filters, importing clip art, and all the tips and tricks for "tracing" bitmap images to convert them into full vector graphics for both photographs and logos. Now we can recreate all of those non-editable images and make them resizable and thus enhance our current design projects.

12
Using the XML Editor

Now we're ready to dig, just a little bit, into some code. We're going to learn about the XML Editor that is included within Inkscape. This feature helps us perform cool tricks that can help with global changes in web development and when working with a programming team that can also create scripts to automatically make some changes.

The goals of this chapter are to:

◆ Learn how to access the XML Editor

◆ Understand the basics of the SVG coding language Inkscape uses (which is an iteration of XML)

◆ Learn how to edit some of the object XML code

◆ Review the essentials for handing off files to make sure the XML/SVG code can be fully-functional and usable for any backend programming that needs to be done.

Let's first learn a bit about the editor.

Inkscape's XML Editor

One of the features that sets Inkscape apart from other vector graphics programs is the XML Editor. The XML Editor is a code-based version of your canvas, all objects, properties, and more. Within the XML Editor, you can change any aspect of the document and see it immediately reflected on your canvas.

The catch here is you need to learn a bit of SVG code in order to be able to do this fun editing. And, if you learn it, you can do *even more* within the XML interface than you can through the main Inkscape interface as it stands today. But, again, it takes a bit of learning on your part to learn SVG attributes and how best to edit them for your needs. To start, you can view the W3C web site (http://www.w3.org/) directly from Inkscape at any time to see the SVG specifications. From the main menu, select **Help** and then **SVG 1.1 Specification**.

Understanding and using the SVG code allows you to create consistent shadows for objects in your web page design without having to fiddle with a number of menus and settings, or create rectangles that always have the same rounded corners—again, without menus, fields and settings. However, let's just start at the beginning and open the XML Editor.

Time for action – accessing the XML Editor

To begin we will open the XML editor in Inkscape:

1. Accessing the XML Editor is the easy part. From any open Inkscape document, on the main menu, select **Edit** and then **XML Editor**.

You can also open the XML Editor using the keyboard shortcut *Shift+Ctrl+X*.

What just happened?

The XML window opened, and if your Inkscape canvas is blank, it will look something like the following screenshot:

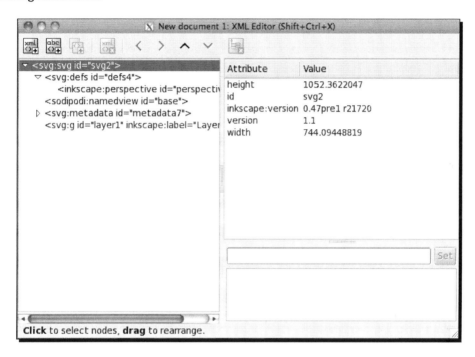

On the left-hand side of this screen is the SVG code and on the right-hand side of the screen you see the attributes and values associated with the selected line of code. You can also select line items on the right-hand side of the screen and reset the values—in essence, editing the code directly.

XML Editor basics

Let's look at a more complicated Inkscape document that is populated with a web design. Then we can discuss the screen basics, the SVG code, and understand how we might be able to edit it for our use. The following screenshot shows the open Inkscape document and the associated SVG code, side-by-side.

As you select items in the SVG code, you will see that Inkscape selects the items in the design (and vice versa). Also, if you were to edit any of the object properties, all changes would happen in real time on the canvas. But let's not get ahead of ourselves. First we need to understand the basics of the XML Editor screen:

- The **structure** or **tree** of the XML is shown on the left-hand side of the screen (see the following screenshot). This XML tree is the entire canvas shown in SVG code.

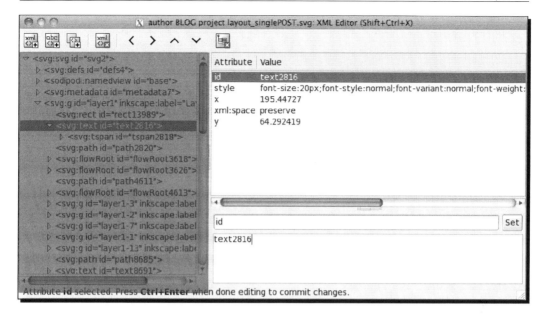

◆   A **layer** is essentially a *node* in the tree. If the layer contained drawn objects, there would be additional nodes embedded beneath the layer node. Each node represents an object on that layer.

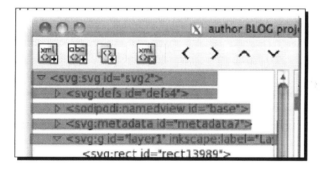

These nodes are expandable by clicking the arrow on the left-hand side. When pointing down, all objects are viewable (and editable). When the arrow is sideways, the objects are hidden.

◆ The **attributes** or **properties** of a selected object are on the right-hand side of the screen. This is where you would edit the properties.

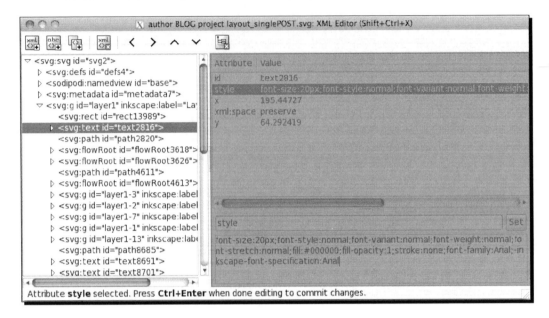

You select an attribute of the object to edit, and then in the bottom portion of the screen, you make your changes and click the **Set** button to commit to the change, as seen in the following screenshot:

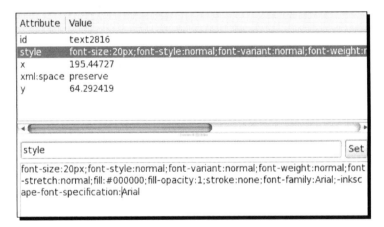

SVG basics

Let's take a step back for a moment and understand the attributes—or the SVG code—found in the XML Editor. We'll still keep it in the context of the Inkscape XML Editor window, so you won't have to know all of the SVG syntax code, but still enough to understand the common attributes and what they mean to your web designs.

Attribute types

First, attributes fall into two categories: those that are SVG standard attributes and then those that can only be found in Inkscape. For those that fall within the SVG standards, they will be recognized by other SVG-rendering programs, and thus can be edited by them as well. However the others—the Inkscape only attributes—are only recognized in Inkscape. What does this mean if you export and use them in other SVG-rendering programs? Not much, they'll just be ignored. Alternatively, you can export the drawing in a way that will not even include these elements.

Thus, when you are saving a document in Inkscape, you are given the option to save as **Inkscape SVG** or **Plain SVG**.

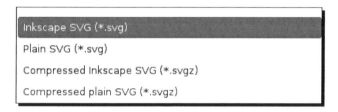

To maintain editability, we recommend saving in **Inkscape SVG**.

How can you can tell which attributes are Inkscape only and which are SVG standard? The **sodipodi** tagis found only on attributes that are Inkscape only. The *sodipodi* tag comes from the roots of the Inkscape application. It was branched from the Sodipodi program and thus the sodipodi tag in the SVG editor.

In the following example, you can see that the icon's width (sodipodi: rx) and height (sodipodi: ry) are both Inkscape-native SVG code. The circle attribute cx gives the exact location of the Circle's Height Transformation node and cy gives the position of the Circle's Width Transformation node.

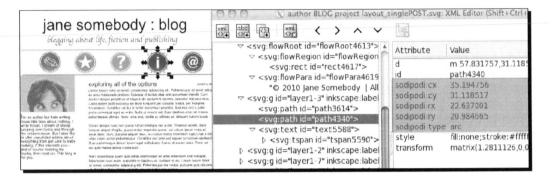

1. How can you can tell which attributes are Inkscape only and which are SVG standard?

   a. The *sodipodi* tag

   b. The rx and ry values

   c. Location on the XML tree

   d. None of the above

Basic attributes

There are books that can explain how best to code and script using SVG. Here, we will aim to give you a very brief overview of the code and how you can *read* it, and the attribute properties.

This isn't intended to show you how to *hand-code* the SVG data, as it is rarely done that way. As with Inkscape, you would use an SVG-authoring environment with a graphical interface that creates most of the code and then you would go in later and edit the attribute information. But even with this, it helps to understand the very basics of the attribute properties and how they are structured.

To start, we will discuss objects. SVG offers four data types to work with; namely, paths, shapes, images, and text. For each of these objects, you have a number of attributes you define to actually create, define, and position the images you see on the canvas.

Paths

In SVG (and Inkscape), paths are outlines of shapes. These paths can be filled (add color) and/or have a stroke associated with them—and thus paths are critical objects to create shapes and other items in Inkscape.

Shapes

How does SVG allow you to create all these *pictures*? Well, each object is made up of a number of shapes. And thus, SVG also uses six predefined shape *elements* within its code for you to manipulate. These basic shape elements are:

- rectangle (rect)
- circle
- ellipse
- line
- polyline
- polygon

Each SVG shape has a number of attributes associated with it and once those attributes are defined, the *code* can be made into an actual shape. Let's go through each of these as an example.

Rectangles have four attributes—x, y, width, and height—which define the placement and dimensions of the rectangle. The x attribute is the distance from the left-hand side of the canvas, the y attribute is the distance from the top of the canvas. Using x and y together, you are defining the top-left corner of the rectangle. This leaves the width and height attributes—and, they define exactly what you would assume: the dimensions of the two dimensional object.

Here's how you would see the code in the XML Editor:

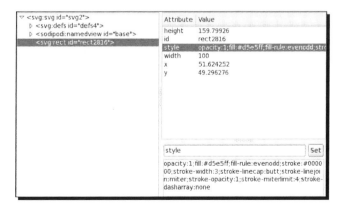

Notice the `rect ID <svg:rect id=rect2816>` is the object information, and is shown on the left-hand side, whereas all of the attributes (`x`, `y`, `height`, and `width`) are shown on the right-hand side. There is also an `id` and `style` attribute which is common to all objects. The `id` attribute is either automatically assigned in Inkscape or set when making the object in the graphical interface (from the main menu, choose **Object | Object Properties).**

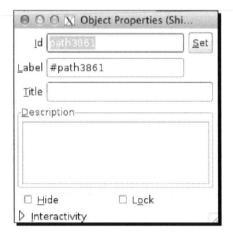

The **Id** field (highlighted above) can be changed and thus reflected in the SVG code.

Back in the XML Editor, the `style` attribute captures all of the color, stroke, opacity, fill information, and more. As you select any attribute, you can see all the details in the bottom of the screen (this is where you would edit that information, too).

What would the rectangle, as seen in this SVG code example, look like? See the following screenshot:

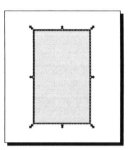

Next let's discuss a circle. It uses the pathid to create it and has four attributes: cx, cy, rx and ry. The cx and cy attributes define the exact center of the circle (placement), while the rx and ry values are the radii of the circle. An example of the SVG code in the **XML Editor** would look similar to the following screenshot:

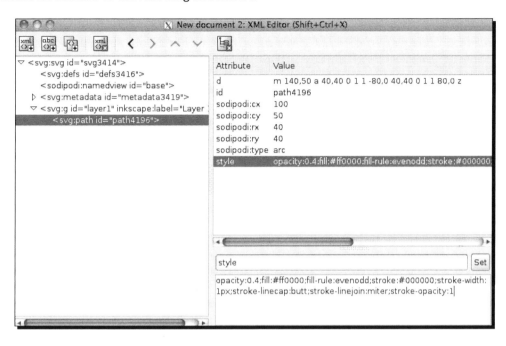

From this code, we see that the center of the circle is at 100, 50 and the circle would have a radius of 40. We can also see from the style attribute that there is color in the circle, but it is at 40 percent capacity and has a stroke outline that is 2 pixels thick.

On the canvas, this all translates into a circle looking similar to the following screenshot:

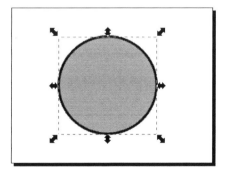

The ellipse is similar to the circle, except that it has four path id attributes in Inkscape: cx, cy, rx, and ry. Again, cx and cy specify the center of the ellipse. The r attributes—rx and ry—give the x-axis and y-axis radii of the ellipse. Again, unless geometry is a favorite pastime, typically you would create this object using the graphical interface and then refine it in the **XML Editor** code. So, let's see what the code would look like:

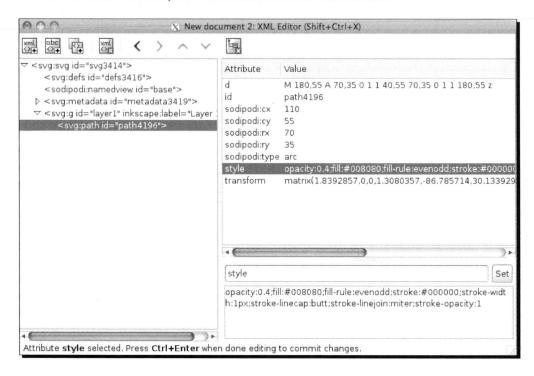

We see here, for this example, the center of the circle is at 110, 55 and it has an x-axis radius of 70 and y-axis radius of 35.

The ellipse would look similar to the following on the canvas:

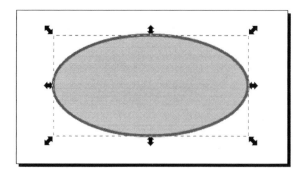

Next up, we will learn about the path object. Essentially, you will map every "point" or node on the object. That means you will have many x and y coordinate pairs in the code for these types of objects. Here's a sample of the code in the XML Editor:

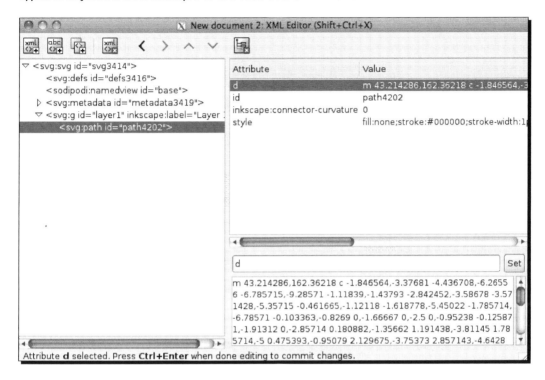

And here is the corresponding line on the canvas:

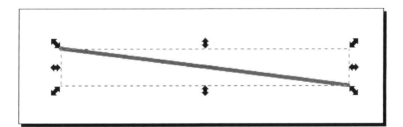

Now for the details about polylines and polygons. The attributes are the same as those of the path object. Every *point* or node on the object is mapped with x and y coordinate pairs in the code for these types of objects.

But what is the difference between polygons and polylines if the attributes are the same (an x and y value for every node of the shape)? It's the stroke outline—for polylines, it doesn't automatically close the shape as the polygon element automatically does.

Here's a simple code example for a polyline (again, this would be the same for a polygon, except the stroke would *close* the shape:

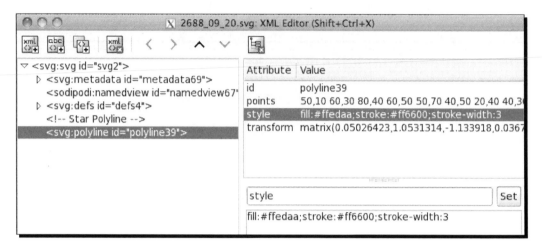

This is how it would look on the canvas:

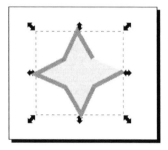

With this example, you can see how difficult it would be to hand-code all of the nodes of the star to make the image. In fact, you would be likely to spend more time trying to find coordinates and mapping them instead of actually drawing the shapes. This is why Inkscape's interface is best for drawing and using the XML Editor to edit or manage some settings which we'll talk about next.

You always have to make sure you have an even number of coordinate values, meaning, for every x value you have, you must specify a corresponding y coordinate. SVG coding programs will prompt you for this and in Inkscape, it is recommended you *draw* the graphics using the interface and then go into the **XML Editor** to change any specific settings.

Images

As you have seen, SVG files are considered the source files for Inkscape. They are graphic images themselves, but they can also contain other graphic formats (such as PNG, JPG, or other SVG files). You can even transform and animate those graphics as well (and even use some scripting to work with them).

In order to do all of that, there is an `image` object in Inkscape. The attributes for it are: `x` and `y`, which again define the top-left corner of the image; `width`, and `height` attributes that give measurements; and the `xlink:href` attribute which defines the actual path or location of the original image. Think of it as the *link* to the original image file, as in HTML code.

A code sample in the **XML Editor** will look similar to the following screenshot:

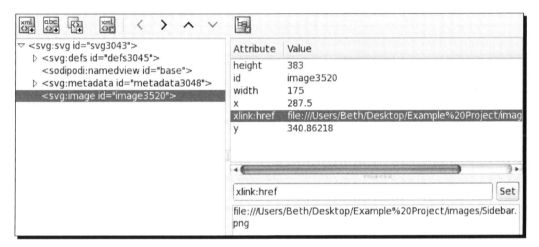

Text

Lastly, as you know from the many examples we have created so far, you can create text in your drawings. Much like the image attribute, there are `x` and `y` values that set the top-left/starting point for your text and then the actual text that is displayed. Here's a sample of what that looks like in the **XML Editor**:

Attribute	Value
id	text3524
sodipodi:linespacing	125%
style	font-size:18;font-style:normal;font-variant:nc
x	107.1901
xml:space	preserve
y	329.31625

```
▽ <svg:svg id="svg3043">
  ▷ <svg:defs id="defs3045">
    <sodipodi:namedview id="base">
  ▷ <svg:metadata id="metadata3048">
    ▼ <svg:text id="text3524">
      ▽ <svg:tspan id="tspan3526">
        "Sample text to show off what you
```

Using the XML Editor to change characteristics

Now, suppose you have created a mock website using the graphical interface of Inkscape and you have handed off all of your files to the programming team. Suddenly, your client decides that they want all heading text to be a specific color of gray (4d4d4d).

Do you have to open each graphic file and make this change? Maybe. But you can also change it right in the **XML Editor** (and if your programmers are using your SVG files directly, they might even be able to make the change).

Time for action – using the XML Editor to change object characteristics

Here's how you would use the XML Editor to change heading text to a specific web color:

1. Open up the **XML Editor** (or an SVG authoring tool) and open your website file.

2. Find the headings you want to change. To do this, find text objects that match what you are looking for. Programmers may have named all of these HeadingXX, where XX is a number to identify each of them.

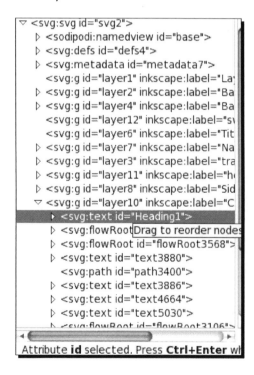

3. Expand the object and find the `style` attribute.

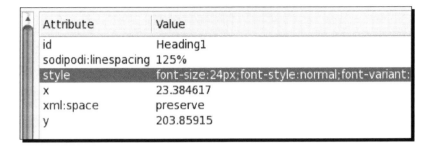

4. Then look for the fill information and change that web color to the new gray one: `4d4d4d`.

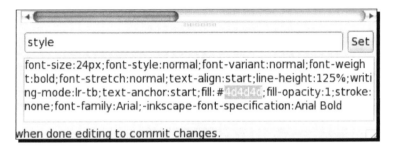

5. Click on **Set**.

What just happened?

You changed the heading text characteristics so that it is now gray in color, as seen in the following screenshot:

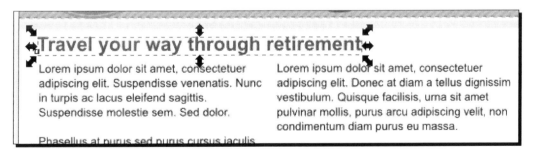

You can even write scripts that are able to automatically search and find all heading IDs (as described in step number 2) and change them! Work with your programming team if you want to learn how to do this. Lots of tools can help you learn the XML/SVG code side of this.

The main use for the **XML Editor** is to correct flaws that cannot be corrected through the interface or through advanced features (which do not have a menu item). An example of this is applying a filter and having the boundaries chopping off a part of the visual output due to the offset. For more examples, see some online tutorials here: `http://tavmjong.free.fr/INKSCAPE/MANUAL/html/XML-Examples.html`

Using XML and graphics with programmers

XML, SVG code, and scripting typically land in the laps of those who actually code the web page. Sometimes they can all be the same person—but in larger corporate or consulting groups, it is a split responsibility. And the one major point to remember is that when you hand off your design mockup files, you include everything!

All SVG source files, all output PNG files, every graphic you used to create the mockup, and more. And in fact, if you created object properties (names) for your layers and objects—give the programming team a cheat sheet of that information as well. All of this will make the transition from web design mockup to real web page easier, cleaner, and more efficient.

Summary

This chapter was full of the technical—XML and SVG code, objects, attributes, x and y values, and more. First we learned how to open the **XML Editor**. Then we took a step back and learned a bit about SVG coding; all about the shape, image, and text attributes. We even dug further into the code a bit to edit some text. Of course, there is a lot more that can be done with the code version of your graphics—but we left most of that to a programming team, or for more investigative work on your part.

Where to Find More Information

If you need help with Inkscape, here are some links to people and places, which will prove invaluable. You can also use the tutorials that are within Inkscape itself. You can find these in the main menu, **Help | Tutorials**.

Official sites

The site that you will find most valuable of all is, of course, the Inkscape homepage at `http://inkscape.org/`. It will provide you with all the manuals, current download release information, forums, and all the information about Inkscape that you might want.

Other important links from the official homepage are as follows:

♦ Manual and documentation: `http://tavmjong.free.fr/INKSCAPE/MANUAL/html/index.html`

♦ Wiki: `http://wiki.inkscape.org/wiki/index.php/Inkscape`

♦ For developers: `https://launchpad.net/inkscape`

♦ Clip Art: `http://www.openclipart.org/`

♦ Galleries: `http://wiki.inkscape.org/wiki/index.php/Galleries`

Articles and tutorials

Inkscape has a number of official tutorials, which the developers helped create, which teach you about the software. You can find these here: `http://inkscape.org/doc/index.php?lang=en`

However, you might like some other self-guided tutorials. You can find some in these locations:

- Inkscape Tutorials weblog: `http://inkscapetutorials.wordpress.com/`
- Floss Manuals: `http://en.flossmanuals.net/Inkscape/`
- 35 Tutorials to create amazing Vector Graphics using Inkscape: `http://speckyboy.com/2009/04/28/35-tutorials-to-create-amazing-vector-graphics-using-inkscape/`

Community

As with many open source programs, there are a number of mailing lists and forums you can join as a user, for more resources. You can find key ones here:

- Official mailing lists: `http://inkscape.org/mailing_lists.php?lang=en`
- Official forums: `http://www.inkscapeforum.com/`
- Inkscape Development Online Discussion: `http://inkscape.org/discussion.php?lang=en`
- User FAQ: `http://wiki.inkscape.org/wiki/index.php/FAQ`

Blogs

There are also a number of blogs and screencasts (video blogs) that teach you how to use Inkscape. You can find my favorites here:

- How-to category: Screencasters.Heathenx.org: `http://screencasters.heathenx.org/`. HeathenX screencasters is a video collection on Inkscape tutorials. He uses an older version of Inkscape, but the tutorials are still useful in learning the basics and some advanced techniques.
- Informational/How-to category: Tavmjong Bah's Blog: `http://tavmjong.free.fr/blog/`

  Tavmjong Bah is a developer for Inkscape and he represents Inkscape in the SVG working group. The blog talks a lot about Inkscape features as well as the SVG applications of the program.

- Design/Graphic category: 365 Sketches: `http://365sketches.org/`

  365 sketches from John LeMasney was a project that started in 2010. The mission was to create a small sketch using Inkscape each day. The site is the result of that project. Through a portion of 2011, he used primarily Inkscape, but more current work is done using GIMP. He used two of my tutorials for response.

Twitter

Here are some of the best Inkscape resources on Twitter:

- For education and tutorials:
    - The official Inkscape twitter feed: `http://twitter.com/inkscape`
    - Inkscape Tutorials: `http://twitter.com/inkscapetuts`

- For design examples:
    - FossGrafis.com: `http://twitter.com/fossgrafis`
    - Linux Artist: `http://twitter.com/linuxartist`

- For fun:
    - Inkscape Mag: `http://twitter.com/inkscapemag`
    - John Lemasney: `http://twitter.com/lemasney`

- For Open Source information: `http://twitter.com/PacktOpenSource`

B
Keyboard Shortcuts

Following are the basic keyboard shortcuts for Inkscape .48 release of the software. For a full list of keyboard shortcuts from the Inkscape developers directly, see `http://inkscape.org/doc/keys048.html`

 If you are using a Macintosh computer, all instances of (Ctrl) should be replaced with the Command (Cmd) key.

You can also download and use a graphical version of the Inkscape Keyboard Layout from `http://Ctrl.openclipart.org/detail/81331`

The list of keyboard shortcuts is given as follows:

Keyboard shortcut	Feature function
File menu shortcuts	
Ctrl + N	Create new document
Ctrl + O	Open an SVG document
Shift + Ctrl + E	Export to PNG
Ctrl + I	Import bitmap or SVG
Ctrl + P	Print document
Ctrl + S	Save document
Shift + Ctrl + S	Save under a new name
Shift + Ctrl + Alt + S	Save a copy
Ctrl + Q	Exit Inkscape

Keyboard shortcut	Feature function
Tools shortcuts	
F1, s	Selector
Space	Switch to the Selector tool temporarily; another *Space* switches back
Shift + F2, Ctrl	Tweak tool
F3, z	Zoom tool
F4, r	Rectangle tool
Shift + F4, x	3D box tool
F5, e	Ellipse/arc tool
F6, p	Freehand (Pencil) tool
Shift + F6, b	Bezier (Pen) tool
Ctrl + F6, c	Calligraphy tool
Shift + F7, u	Paint Bucket tool
Ctrl + F1, g	Gradient tool
F7, d	Dropper tool
F8, t	Text tool
F9, i	Spiral tool
Shift + F9	Star tool
Ctrl + F2, o	Connector tool
Dialog windows	
Shift + Ctrl + F	Fill and Stroke
Shift + Ctrl + W	Swatches
Shift + Ctrl + T	Text and Font
Shift + Ctrl + M	Transform
Shift + Ctrl + L	Layers
Shift + Ctrl + A	Align and Distribute
Shift + Ctrl + O	Object Properties
Shift + Ctrl + H	Undo History
Shift + Ctrl + X	XML Editor
Shift + Ctrl + D	Document Preferences

Keyboard shortcut	Feature function
Dialog windows	
Shift + Ctrl + P	Inkscape Preferences
Shift + Ctrl + E	Export to PNG
Ctrl + F	Find
Shift + Alt + B	Trace Bitmap
Shift + Ctrl + 7	Path Effects
Basic object shortcuts	
Shift + Ctrl + Y, Ctrl + Z	Undo
Shift + Ctrl + Z, Ctrl + Y	Redo
Ctrl + C	Copy selection
Ctrl + X	Cut selection
Ctrl + V	Paste clipboard
Ctrl + Alt + V	Paste in place
Shift + Ctrl + V	Paste style
Ctrl + 7	Paste path effect
Ctrl + D	Duplicate selection
Alt + D	Clone object
Shift + Alt + D	Unlink clone
Shift + D	Select original
Alt + B	Create a bitmap copy
Shift + Alt + B	Trace bitmap
Alt + I	Object(s) to pattern
Shift + Alt + I	Pattern to object(s)
Shift + Ctrl + U, Ctrl + G	Group selected objects
Shift + Ctrl + G, Ctrl + U	Ungroup selected group(s)
Home	Raise selection to top
End	Lower selection to bottom
PageUp	Raise selection one step
PageDown	Lower selection one step

Glossary of Terms

Alignment makes sure all of the elements line up on the screen. Use natural alignments within an entire web space when you use more than one graphical element such as photos, graphics, and/or text.

Attributes are the properties of an object, as seen in the Inkscape XML editor. Selecting an attribute (such as stroke or fill) will then let you see the detailed properties (such as color codes and line thicknesses).

Backgrounds are "behind" the overall design of a web page. They can be any design, shape, size, or color, but as a rule of thumb, should not distract from the overall design of a web page.

Blogs, now commonplace on the web, are websites or portions of websites that offer commentary on personal events, politics, videos, pictures, and anything else that can be "posted" online. The structure of blogs is around posts that are published in reverse-chronological order and allow readers to provide comments and sometimes ratings.

Buttons are used on forms found in web pages where a user needs to "submit" information that will be stored.

Canvas is the page or document in Inkscape where your objects and shapes are created.

Cascading Style Sheet (CSS) is used with the HTML/XML coding to define the look and formatting of an entire website. One style sheet determines fonts, colors, spacing, placement, and more, reducing complexity and repetition in the coding of the pages themselves.

Contrast is a state of being different from something else, for example, abstractly different sizes, colors, directions, shapes and fonts (for example mixing modern with old style), font weights, and more.

Diagram is a graphical representation of information that uses shapes, images, and more to create a cohesive thought. There are a number of diagram types like Venn, Activity, Tree, Network, and more.

Dialogs are vernacularly used in Inkscape to describe specific windows or portions of the screens.

Extensions in the world of Inkscape are like scripts. They are created, installed, and then incorporated into the Inkscape software itself to "extend" the software's features or functionality.

Fill is the terminology to describe the color of an object or shape.

Font when using text, it specifies a certain size and style of type.

Flow Chart is one of the most common types of diagrams. It shows the general process for completing a task or decision. It shows each step, decision, and option as a particular box/option/connector. In general, it represents a step-by-step solution to a given problem.

GIMP (GNU Image Manipulation Program) is an open source photo manipulation software program. This is used in this book for the process of creating an animated GIF. More information can be found at: http://www.gimp.org.

Grid is a tool in Inkscape to help alignment and exact measurements. It can be particularly useful in creating web page designs because there are "snap to grid" options to help with exact alignment.

Guides are also tools in Inkscape in Inkscape that can be user-generated. You can create guides on your canvas to help with alignment and object placement.

Handle is a term used to describe small squares or circles at edges of an object in Inkscape. Handles are often used to change the size of an object or change the shape of a path.

Icons is a graphical representation of text, usually smaller objects that represent a certain feature or function on a web page. They can be completely graphical or a combination of graphics and text.

Layers in the Inkscape software allow stacking of objects on a canvas for easier creation. Each layer can be locked, viewed, moved, and more. You must select a layer before you can start manipulating objects within that layer. This selected layer is then termed the drawing layer.

Lock is used to lock objects, shapes, text, and layers in Inkscape. Once this setting is in place, these objects become un-editable until unlocked.

Logo is a visual representation of a company or brand.

Lorem Ipsum is a text effect that displays a pseudo-Latin form of text that is used as a "placeholder" in the larger context of the web page design. It allows visual correlation of text content, without having to create actual text for that space in the design.

Open Clip Art Library is an open source, free clip art image library that you can search directly from Inkscape.

Organizational Chart or "org chart" shows the structure of an organization. It also details roles, job titles, and sometimes the relationships between the jobs.

Panning is moving left, right, or up and down on the Inkscape main screen.

Paths in general terms, are lines that have a start and end point, curves, angles, and points that are calculated by a mathematical equation. However, paths are not limited to being straight—they can be of any shape, size, and can even encompass any number of curves. When you combine them, they create drawings, diagrams, and can even help create certain fonts.

Plugins are additional software that you install to add new capabilities to Inkscape.

Properties define details regarding an object created in Inkscape. These are typically editable and can be changed with the software interface or within the XML editor.

Proximity is a design term used to describe grouping of similar information together on a web page.

Rasterized images are images that are created by tiny rectangular dots, which we call pixels. File types like JPG, FIG, and BMP are all rasterized images.

Repetition the idea of repeating elements like buttons, shapes (graphical or just placement), or colors in a design to make a pleasing impact.

RSS (Really Simple Syndication) feeds is a basic way to continually broadcast (or publish) blog entries. These feeds are in a standardized XML format and pull the metadata tags you assigned when publishing your blog post and display them in "readers" for others to automatically receive.

Scalable Vector Graphics or SVG is a vector-based drawing language that uses some basic principles: it can be scalable to any size without losing detail, and a drawing can use an unlimited number of smaller drawings used in any number of ways (and reused) and still be a part of a larger whole.

Scan is a process Inkscape uses to describe a "pass" over a bitmap image in order to create a trace of the image. Single scans are done with a single pass (or scan) to create the paths. Multiple scans, in turn, use multiple passes using different settings each time to create different paths that are then stored and displayed in a group to create the trace.

Scripts add new features to Inkscape. They must be installed after the initial Inkscape installation and are typically written in a different programming language from the main program (Inkscape, in this case) and can be modified at any time.

Shapes in Inkcape and SVG, are basic shape elements; these include rectangles, circles, ellipses, straight lines, polylines, and polygons. They have different attributes from paths, and can have fill and stroke information edited via the software interface as well as with the XML editor directly.

SIOX (Simple Interactive Object Extraction) is a process of separating an object from the background in a bitmap image.

Site tree/Site Map is a list of all the individual pages of a website. Typically, the site map outlines how each page is linked to the others. It can be used for website creation and, planning, but also as a user interface aide to help website users find where they need to be on the site.

Storefronts are any websites that sell a commodity. They often allow you to search through products and then purchase a product through a "shopping cart".

Stroke is the term in Inkscape to describe an object or shape border. You can often change the stroke color and thickness.

Template is a base document that has been created to simplify the design process. Basic settings like canvas size, fonts, colors, and placement are pre-defined and set in the document.

Text styling is the term used to describe manipulating text, so that it creates a certain feel when seen in an overall design. Sometimes it is also called typography or typesetting.

Tracing is the process of creating paths (and nodes) to represent an underlying bitmap image and then using those paths to create a vector-based image.

Vector graphics is the use of points, lines, curves, and shapes or polygons, which are all based on mathematical equations to represent images in computer graphics.

Wallpapers are images used as desktop backgrounds. These are also commonly used (and downloaded) for use with cell phones and other electronic devices.

XML Editor is the code-based version of objects and drawings on your Inkscape canvas. Within the XML Editor, you can change any aspect of the document and see it immediately reflected on your canvas.

Zoom describes magnifying your canvas to see more detail (zoomed in) or the entire canvas at a glance (zoomed out).

Pop Quiz Answers

Chapter 1, Getting Started with Vector Graphics

Pop quiz – understanding vector graphics

1	d

Chapter 2, Installing and Opening Inkscape

Pop quiz – using Tools

1	d
	This is the most used toolbar in Inkscape because it gives you the tools to create shapes, paths, and more. All you have to do is select (click) a tool and then use it on the open document page.

1	c
	Click the new document icon on the command bar. It just takes one click!

Chapter 3, How to Manage Files

Pop quiz – how do you change the dimensions of a predefined graphic

1	c
	Just adjust the document dimensions of the current document to fit your needs.
	Remember, you'll likely also need to move objects on your page to reflect the new dimensions.
	However, for any of the objects that you have drawn, there will be no stretching or manipulation.
	The page dimensions just change (the black borders).

Pop quiz – editable Inkscape file formats

1	b
	You can also save in the Inkscape compressed format of SVGZ if minimizing the file size is important.

Pop quiz – Export versus Save As

1	c
	Inkscape only supports exporting PNG files. However, the File	Save/Save As function will allow you to save files as PDFs.

Pop quiz – file format portability

1	d
	PDF files, when imported into Inkscape, allow for editability to remain with vector-based objects.

Pop quiz – linking versus embedding images

1	d

Chapter 4, Creating your First Graphics

Pop quiz – displaying borders

1	a
	Since a border is essentially the end of your graphic you can use it for a number of purposes—most importantly to show the boundary for where you can create graphics that will be printed or exported when your file is saved.

Pop quiz – switching shapes

1	c
	You would use the toolbox and select the cube icon (6th icon from the top).

Pop quiz – image formats

1	d

Pop quiz – circles

1	c
	Use the circle tool in the toolbox and press the *Ctrl* key while resizing it.

Pop quiz – joining objects

1	a
	Make sure all of the objects are selected on your canvas that you want to join together in a union first and then select Path | Union. More details about this, grouping, and combining paths will be discussed in *Chapter 7, Creating paths into complex shapes" to "Using Paths"*

Pop quiz – deleting

1	d

Pop quiz – viewable grid

1	c

Chapter 5, How to Work with Layers

Pop quiz – Layers dialog

1	b

Pop quiz – background colors

1	c
	All Inkscape files are transparent by default. We had set the document properties to have a white solid background for our web design mockup so that it would be consistent with how the web page would be coded.

Pop quiz – undo last action

1	a

Chapter 6, Building Objects

Pop quiz – changing Fill and Stroke

TRUE or FALSE: No matter what way you use to change fill and stroke of an object in Inkscape, it all has the same outcome for the object on your canvas.	TRUE. By using the Fill and Stroke dialog, the dropper tool, or the color palette you are changing the same attributes on the object.

Pop quiz – shortcut keys to quickly ungroup items

1	d

Chapter 7, Using Paths

Pop quiz – remove the last node movement

1	d
	Either using the keyboard shortcut *Ctrl + Z* or Edit | Undo works!

Pop quiz – paths

1	d
	Almost any object you create in Inkscape can be converted to a path so you can add effects or move nodes to get the desired effect

Chapter 8, How to Style Text

Pop quiz – font options

1	e
	There is no option to underline in Inkscape. Instead you can use other tools to draw a line under any text you wish to have underlined.

Pop Quiz – transparency

1	b
	It is actually transparent. For a mask to work, like in the example in this chapter, you need to change the Alpha setting to white. Masking takes the shades of gray onto the "bottom" object. If the Alpha setting was set at transparent then the reflection would also be transparent.

Chapter 9, Using Filters

Pop quiz – common icon sizes

1	b
	All the others listed can be seen in the icon preview option in Inkscape (View | Icon Preview).

Chapter 10, Extensions in Inkscape

Pop quiz – what are extensions?

TRUE OR FALSE: Extensions add new capabilities to Inkscape and thus extend its features or functionality and on their own, outside of their use in Inkscape, wouldn't work correctly.	TRUE. Most Inkscape extensions are created using Python or Perl programming languages.

Chapter 11, Working with Images

Pop quiz – Open Clip Art

1	d
	You can indeed use any image from the Open Clip Art Library in your work—all are downloadable in SVG format, editable, and you can adjust them as necessary for your own designs.

Chapter 12, Using the XML Editor

Pop quiz – sodipodi tag

1	a
	The sodipodi tag is the only one attribute that is Inkscape-only. It comes from the roots of the Inkscape application which was branched from the Sodipodi program, and thus the sodipodi tag in the SVG editor.

Index

Symbols

3D box tool 254
365 Sketches blog, Design/Graphic Category 250
.ai. *See* Adobe Illustrator
.eps. *See* Encapsulated Post Script file
.Fhx. *See* Adobe Freehand
.pdf. *See* Adobe Acrobat Portable Document
         Format
.psd. *See* Adobe Photoshop
.svg file 9
.svg format 9, 10

A

Add Layer dialog 108
Adobe Acrobat Portable Document Format 9
Adobe Freehand 9
Adobe Illustrator 9
Adobe Photoshop 9
Align and Distribute dialog 94, 96, 168, 224, 254
Align and Distribute Objects icon 94, 224
alignment 257
Alt + B 255
Alt + D 255
Alt + I 255
Alt + [or] keys, hot keys 176
Alt + > or < keys, hot keys 176
Alt + right or left arrows, hot keys 176
Alt + Shift + arrows, hot keys 176
arc
   creating, steps 75-78

attributes
   about 257
   types 237
attributes, XML editor screen 236

B

b 254
Background layer 99
backgrounds 257
basic object shortcuts, keyboard shortcuts
   Alt + B 255
   Alt + D 255
   Alt + I 255
   Ctrl + 7 255
   Ctrl + Alt + V 255
   Ctrl + C 255
   Ctrl + D 255
   Ctrl + V 255
   Ctrl + X 255
   End 255
   Home 255
   PageDown 255
   PageUp 255
   Shift + Alt + B 255
   Shift + Alt + D 255
   Shift + Alt + I 255
   Shift + Ctrl + CTRL, Ctrl + Z 255
   Shift + Ctrl + G, Ctrl + U 255
   Shift + Ctrl + U, Ctrl + G 255
   Shift + Ctrl + V 255
   Shift + D 255

batch images
  exporting 52-54
Bezier (Pen) 66, 82
Bezier tool
  about 84, 254
  womans face shape, creating 146
bitmap
  tracing 255
bitmap copy
  creating 255
blend mode
  about 112
  using, steps 112, 113
Blend mode drop-down menu 113
Blend mode option 112
blogs, InkScape
  365 Sketches, Design/Graphic Category 250
  about 257
  Screencasters.Heathenx.org, How-To category 250
  Tavmjong Bah's Blog, Informational/How-to Category 250
  URL 21
blur 123
Blur slider 226
borders
  displaying, pop quiz answers 263
brochure files
  building 14, 15
buttons 257

C

c 254
Calligraphy tool 66, 254
canvas 257
Cascading Style Sheet. *See* **CSS**
CD cover
  creating 37, 38
Center on Vertical Axis icon 95
circle tool
  about 112
  pop quiz answers 264
clip art
  URL 21, 249

clipboard
  pasting 255
clipping
  about 133
  objects 133-141
clone
  object 255
  unlink 255
closed paths 66
color palette bar
  about 126
  pop quiz answers 265
  using, steps 126, 127
community, InkScape
  Inkscape Development Online Discussion, URL 250
  official forums, URL 250
  official mailing lists, URL 250
  User FAQ, URL 250
compound paths 66
connector tool 254
contrast 257
Create and Edit Objects tool 94
Create and Edit tool 94
CSS 257
Ctrl 254
Ctrl + 7 255
Ctrl + Alt + V 255
Ctrl + B, hot keys 176
Ctrl + C 255
Ctrl + D 255
Ctrl + F 255
Ctrl + F1 254
Ctrl + F2 254
Ctrl + F6 254
Ctrl + I 253
Ctrl + I, hot keys 176
Ctrl + left/right arrows, keyboard shortcuts 176
Ctrl + N 253
Ctrl + O 253
Ctrl + [or], hot keys 176
Ctrl + P 253
Ctrl + Q 253
Ctrl + S 253
Ctrl + Shift + Home, keyboard shortcuts
  about 176
  for Mac OS 176

Ctrl + Shift + left/right arrows, keyboard
    shortcuts 176
Ctrl + V 255
Ctrl + X 255
current layer 103
cut path, path option 167

D

d 254
Dashes field 125
deleting
  pop quiz answers 264
diagram 258
dialog boxes
  closing 31
  displaying 31
  floating 31
  minimizing 31
  multiple dialog boxes, displaying 31
dialogs 258
dialog windows, keyboard shortcuts
  Ctrl + F 255
  Shift + Alt + B 255
  Shift + Ctrl + 7 255
  Shift + Ctrl + A 254
  Shift + Ctrl + D 254
  Shift + Ctrl + E 255
  Shift + Ctrl + F 254
  Shift + Ctrl + L 254
  Shift + Ctrl + M 254
  Shift + Ctrl + O 254
  Shift + Ctrl + P 255
  Shift + Ctrl + T 254
  Shift + Ctrl + X 254
difference, path option 166
Distribute Centers Equidistantly Horizontally
    button 96
division, path option 166
DMG file 19
Dockable dialogs
  about 30, 31
  floating 33
document
  customizd default document, creating 51
  customized default document, creating 50

printing 253
saving 253
documentation
  URL 249
document dimensions
  custom file size, creating for postcard 39-41
  customizing 39
  print bleed, adding 43
  print-safe border, adding 41-43
Document Preferences 254
Document Properties window 68
Double-click on letters, keyboard shortcuts 176
drawing
  exporting 47
drawing layer 26, 90
dropper
  about 127
  using, steps 128
Dropper tool 254

E

e 254
Edit Paths by Nodes tool 147, 150, 153, 161
ellipse
  about 74, 112
  creating 74
Ellipse/arc tool 254
embedding
  about 59
  logo, into design 59, 60
embedding images
  versus linking 62
Encapsulated Post Script file 9
End 255
exclusion, path option 166
Export Bitmap option 47
exporting
  drawing 47
  page 47
  selection 47
  to PNG 47, 48
  versus save as 49
  versus save as, pop quiz answers 262
extensions
  about 213, 214, 258
  installation 215

pop quiz answers 267
tutorials, examples 214, 215
URL 214

F

F1 254
F3 254
F4 254
F5, e 254
F6 254
F7 254
F8 254
F9 254
file formats
  pop quiz, answers 262
  portability, pop quiz answers 263
file menu shortcuts, keyboard shortcuts
  Ctrl + I 253
  Ctrl + N 253
  Ctrl + O 253
  Ctrl + P 253
  Ctrl + Q 253
  Ctrl + S 253
  Shift + Ctrl + Alt + S 253
  Shift + Ctrl + E 253
  Shift + Ctrl + S 253
files
  creating 35
  embedding 59
  embedding, in Inkscape 59
  linking 58
  pop quiz, answers 262
  predefined-sized document dimensions, using
    36, 37
fill 258
Fill and Stroke dialog
  about 121-124, 167, 195, 226, 254
  blur 123
  color picker 122, 123
  opacity 123
  pop quiz answers 265
  type of fill 122
  using, steps 121
Fill tab 122, 126
filter editor 192

filters
  about 191
  pop quiz answers 267
  using 193-196
  using, with images 199-201
  using, with text 197, 198
find 255
find and replace
  performing, steps 182
flipcase, text effects 184
Floss Manuals
  URL 250
flow chart 258
font 258
font options
  pop quiz answers 266
for developers
  URL 21
forums
  URL 21
freehand object
  lightening bolt, closing 83
  lightening bolt, creating 82, 83
freehand tool 82, 254

G

g 254
galleries
  URL 21, 249
geometrical primitives 65
GIMP 258
GNU General Public License. *See* **GPL**
GNU Image Manipulation Program. *See* **GIMP**
GPL 17
Gradient tool 254
grid
  about 258
  pop quiz answers 264
  viewing 84
Group selected objects 255
guides
  about 258
  creating 87, 88

H

handle 258
height attribute 239
Help | Tutorials 249
Home 255
homepage, InkScape
  clip art, URL 249
  for developers, URL 249
  galleries, URL 249
  manual and documentation, URL 249
  wiki, URL 249
hot keys
  Alt + [or] keys 176
  Alt + > or < keys 176
  Alt + right or left arrows 176
  Alt + Shift + arrows 176
  Alt + Up or down arrows 176
  Ctrl + B 176
  Ctrl + I 176
  Ctrl + [or] 176

I

i 254
icon
  about 258
  creating 167-169
icon sizes
  pop quiz answers 267
Icon View option 170
id attribute 240
image files
  embedding 59
  image embedding, limitations 59
  linking 58
image formats
  pop quiz answers 263
image object 245
images
  about 245
  filters, using 199-201
  tracing 201
  tracing, potrace used 202-204
Import From Open Clip Art Library dialog box
  218

Inkscape
  about 7
  arc, creating 75-78
  blogs 250
  community 250
  dialog box, closing 31
  dialog boxes, displaying 31
  dialog box, floating 31
  dialog box, minimizing 31
  dockable dialogs 30, 31
  document, opening 67, 68
  downloading 19, 20
  drawing layer 26
  ellipse, creating 74
  extensions 213
  external files, linking 61
  exiting 253
  features 17, 18
  files, embedding 59
  filters 191
  getting started 22-25
  grid, viewing 84, 85
  guides, creating 87, 88
  Help | Tutorials 249
  homepage 249
  homepage, URL 21, 249
  installation, troubleshooting 20, 21
  installing 18
  keyboard shortcuts 253
  layout information 26
  logo, embedding in design 59, 60
  main screen 28
  multiple dialog box, displaying 31
  notification area 26
  objects 115
  opacity setting 26
  PDF, importing 56-58
  pointer or cursor position 27
  pop quiz, answers 261
  pre-requisites 18
  running on Mac OS X, requisite 18
  shape options, changing 70, 71
  shapes, combining 78-81
  software basics 21
  star, creating 69, 70
  style Indicator 25

SVG, files saving in 44
SVG, saving 45, 46
templates 210
tutorials 249
tutorials, examples 214, 215
twitter, resources on 251
unit of measure, changing 86
vector graphic, creating 67
vector graphic, saving 72, 73
website, URL 19
window resize 27
XML editor 231, 232
zoom tool 27

Inkscape Development Online Discussion
URL 250
Inkscape, external files linking
photograph, linking into brochure design 61, 62
Inkscape file
non-native Inkscape files, importing 55
saving 44
saving, as PDF 49
saving, in Inkscape SVG 44
Inkscape Preferences 255
Inkscape SVG
about 237
files, saving in 44
saving 45, 46
Inkscape Tutorials weblog
URL 250
intersection, path option 166

K

kerning
about 173
text 174, 175
keyboard shortcuts
basic object shortcuts 255
Ctrl + left/right arrows 176
Ctrl + Shift + End 176
  for Mac OS 176
Ctrl + Shift + Home 176
Ctrl + Shift + left/right arrows 176
dialog windows 254, 255
Double-click on letters 176
file menu shortcuts 253
from developers, URL 253

graphical version, URL 253
Shift + End 176
Shift + Home 176
Shift + left/right arrows 176
tools shortcuts 254
Triple-click 176

L

last node movement
pop quiz answers 266
Layer 1 92
Layer name field 92, 108
layers
about 89, 90, 254, 258
arranging 105
creating, steps 91, 92
deleting 110
deleting, steps 110, 111
dialog 92
drawing layer 90
duplicating 104
duplicating, steps 104
hiding 99
hiding, steps 100-103
locking, steps 98, 99
moving 105-107
nested 108
objects, moving from one layer to another 109
pop quiz answers 264
renaming 109
renaming, steps 109
using, in example drawing 93
using, in web design 93-96
Layers dialog 91
Layers icon 91
layout information 26
lightening bolt example, freehand object
closing 83
creating 82, 83
linking
about 58
versus embedding images 62
versus embedding images, pop quiz answers 263
lock 258
logo 258

Lorem Ipsum 259
Lower selection one step 255
Lower selection to bottom 255

M

mailing list
  URL 21
manual
  URL 249
manual and documentation
  URL 21
masking
  about 133
  objects 142, 143
Multiply blend 114

N

non-vector formats
  vector graphics, disadvantages 11
notification area 26

O

o 254
object characteristics
  changing, XML Editor used 246-248
Object Properties 254
objects
  about 115
  converting, to paths 163-165
  creating 116
  creating, steps 116-120
  grouping, steps 129-132
  masking 142, 143
  pop quiz answers 264
  rotating 80
  transforming, into paths 155
Object(s) to pattern 255
object to path 163-165
official forums
  URL 250
official mailing lists
  URL 250
opacity
  about 123
  setting 26

Open Clip Art Library
  about 18, 217, 259
  pop quiz answers 267
  uses 218
  using (Mac users only) 218, 219
open paths 66
open-standard vector format
  advantages 10
  SVG vector images, advantages 10
org chart. *See* organizational chart
organizational chart 259
original
  selecting 255

P

p 254
page
  exporting 47
PageDown 255
PageUp 255
Paint Bucket tool 254
panning 259
pasting
  in place 255
  path effect 255
  style 255
path effects 255
pathid attributes 242
path options
  about 166
  cut path 167
  difference 166
  division 166
  exclusion 166
  intersection 166
  union 166
paths
  about 66, 239, 259
  Bezier (Pen) 66
  Bezier tool, using 146
  Calligraphy tool 66
  closed paths 66
  compound paths 66
  creating, ways 66
  open paths 66

Pencil (Freehand) 66
pop quiz answers 266
using, for text 177-179
working with 145, 146
Pattern to object(s) 255
PDF
importing, into Inkscape 56-58
Pencil (Freehand) 66
Pencil tool 254
Pen tool 254
photo manipulation
about 219
background, blurring 220-227
photograph, blurring 220-227
Plain SVG 237
plugins 259
PNG
exporting to 47, 48, 253, 255
pointer or cursor position 27
polygons
and polylines, differences 243
creating, steps for 67
polylines
and polygons, differences 243
pop quiz
answers 261-268
postcard
new custom file size, creating 39-41
potrace
about 201
used, for tracing images 202-204
predefined-sized document dimensions
using 36, 37
print bleed
adding 43
print-safe border
adding 41- 43
project files
batch images, exporting 52-54
multiple file projects, managing 52
structuring 51
properties 259
properties, XML editor screen 236
proximity 259

R

r 254
Raise selection one step 255
Raise selection to top 255
random case, text effects 184
rasterized graphics
usage determining 11-13
rasterized images
about 259
versus vector 13, 14
raster logos
converting, to vector-based image 228
converting, to vector-based logos 228
Really Simple Syndication. *See* **RSS feed**
rectangle tool 254
redo 255
reflection
creating 185-188
Rename Layer dialog 110
repetition 259
RSS feed 259

S

s 254
save as
versus export 49
Scalable Vector Graphics. *See* **SVG**
scans 259
Screencasters.Heathenx.org blog, How-To cat-egory
URL 250
Scribus 8
scripts 260
Search for
field 218
selection
copying 255
cutting 255
duplicate 255
exporting 47
selector 254
sentence case, text effects 183

shapes
  about 78, 239, 260
  circle 239
  closed shape, text placing within 179, 180
  combining 78-81
  ellipse 239
  line 239
  options, changing 70, 71
  polygon 239
  polyline 239
  pop quiz answers 263
  rectangle 239
  switching 69, 70
Shift + Alt + B 255
Shift + Alt + D 255
Shift + Alt + I 255
Shift + Ctrl + 7 255
Shift + Ctrl + A 254
Shift + Ctrl + Alt + S 253
Shift + Ctrl + CTRL, Ctrl + Z 255
Shift + Ctrl + D 254
Shift + Ctrl + E 253, 255
Shift + Ctrl + F 254
Shift + Ctrl + G, Ctrl + U 255
Shift + Ctrl + L 254
Shift + Ctrl + M 254
Shift + Ctrl + O 254
Shift + Ctrl + P 255
Shift + Ctrl + S 253
Shift + Ctrl + T 254
Shift + Ctrl + U, Ctrl + G 255
Shift + Ctrl + V 255
Shift + Ctrl + X 254
Shift + D 255
Shift + End, keyboard shortcuts
  about 176
  for Mac OS 176
Shift + F2 254
Shift + F4 254
Shift + F6 254
Shift + F7 254
Shift + F9 254
Shift + Home, keyboard shortcuts
  about 176
  for MAC OS 176

Shift + left/right arrows, keyboard shortcuts 176
Simple Interactive Object Extraction. *See* SIOX
SIOX 201, 205, 206, 260
site map 260
site tree 260
sodipodi tag
  pop quiz answers 268
space 254
spiral tool 254
star
  creating 69, 70
star tool 254
storefronts 260
stroke
  about 260
  to paths 155
Stroke paint tab 124
stroke to paths
  about 155
  spiros and swirls, creating 155-162
structure, XML editor screen 234
style attribute 241
style Indicator 25
SVG
  about 9, 18, 259
  exporting to 253
  open-standard vector format, advantages 10
SVG basics
  about 237
  attribute types 237, 238
  basic attributes 238
SVG document
  opening 253
SVG vector images
  advantages, over open standard vector formats
    10
swatches 254

T

t 254
Tavmjong Bah's Blog, Informational/How-to
  Category 250
templates
  about 210, 260
  custom template, creating 213
  custom templates, creating 212

existing template, modifying 212, 213
installing 210
installing, steps 211
text
  about 245
  filters, using with 197, 198
  path, using for 177-179
  placing, within closed shape 179, 180
Text and Font 254
text and font editor
  about 171
  opening 172
  using 172, 173
text effects
  about 182
  flipcase 184
  random case 184
  sentence case 183
  title case 183
  uppercase and lowercase 183
  using, steps 183
text styling 260
text tool (A icon) 172, 254
T icon 172
title case, text effect 183
tools shortcuts, keyboard shortcuts
  b 254
  c 254
  Ctrl 254
  Ctrl + F1 254
  Ctrl + F2 254
  Ctrl + F6 254
  d 254
  e 254
  F1 254
  F3 254
  F4 254
  F5 254
  F6 254
  F7 254
  F8 254
  F9 254
  g 254
  i 254
  o 254
  p 254
  r 254
  s 254
  Shift + F2 254
  Shift + F4 254
  Shift + F6 254
  Shift + F7 254
  Shift + F9 254
  space 254
  t 254
  u 254
  x 254
  z 254
Trace Bitmap dialog box 228
tracing 260
transform 254
transparency
  pop quiz answers 266
tree, XML editor screen 234
Triple-click, keyboard 176
tutorials, InkScape
  Floss Manuals, URL 250
  Inkscape Tutorials weblog, URL 250
  Vector Graphics, 35 tutorials for creating 250
tweak tool 254
twitter resources, InkScape
  for design examples 251
  for education and tutorials 251
  for fun 251
  for open source information 251

U

u 254
undo 255
Undo History 254
undo last action
  pop quiz answers 265
Ungroup selected group(s) 255
union, path option 166
unit of measure, changing 86
uppercase and lowercase, text effect 183
User FAQ
  URL 250

V

vector-based logos
  raster logos, converting to 228
vector formats 9

vector graphics
about 8, 260
Adobe InDesign 8
brochure files, building 14, 15
characteristics 8
creating 9, 67
disadvantages over non-vector formats 11
new document, opening 67, 68
polygon, creating 67
pop quiz, answers 261
Quark Xpress 8
saving 72, 73
Scribus 8
shape options, changing 70, 71
star, creating 69, 70
usage determining 11, 13
used, by programs 8
versus rasterized images 13, 14

W

wallpapers 260
web design
layers, using 93-96
width attribute 239

wiki
URL 21, 249
window resize 27

X

x 254
xlink:href attribute 245
XML editor
about 231, 232, 254, 260
accessing, steps for 232, 233
basics 234
pop quiz answers 268
screen 234
using, to change object characteristics 246,
247, 248
XML editor screen
attributes 236
layer 235
properties 236
structure 234
tree 234

Z

z 254
zoom tool 27, 254, 260

Thank you for buying
Inkscape *Beginner's Guide*

About Packt Publishing

Packt, pronounced 'packed', published its first book "*Mastering phpMyAdmin for Effective MySQL Management*" in April 2004 and subsequently continued to specialize in publishing highly focused books on specific technologies and solutions.

Our books and publications share the experiences of your fellow IT professionals in adapting and customizing today's systems, applications, and frameworks. Our solution based books give you the knowledge and power to customize the software and technologies you're using to get the job done. Packt books are more specific and less general than the IT books you have seen in the past. Our unique business model allows us to bring you more focused information, giving you more of what you need to know, and less of what you don't.

Packt is a modern, yet unique publishing company, which focuses on producing quality, cutting-edge books for communities of developers, administrators, and newbies alike. For more information, please visit our website: www.packtpub.com.

About Packt Open Source

In 2010, Packt launched two new brands, Packt Open Source and Packt Enterprise, in order to continue its focus on specialization. This book is part of the Packt Open Source brand, home to books published on software built around Open Source licences, and offering information to anybody from advanced developers to budding web designers. The Open Source brand also runs Packt's Open Source Royalty Scheme, by which Packt gives a royalty to each Open Source project about whose software a book is sold.

Writing for Packt

We welcome all inquiries from people who are interested in authoring. Book proposals should be sent to author@packtpub.com. If your book idea is still at an early stage and you would like to discuss it first before writing a formal book proposal, contact us; one of our commissioning editors will get in touch with you.

We're not just looking for published authors; if you have strong technical skills but no writing experience, our experienced editors can help you develop a writing career, or simply get some additional reward for your expertise.

Inkscape 0.48 Illustrator's Cookbook

ISBN: 978-1-84951-266-4   Paperback: 340 pages

109 recipes to create scalable vector graphics with Inkscape

1. Create interesting illustrations and common web design elements that can be used in real-life projects

2. Gain a thorough understanding of all common Inkscape tools and advanced features of Inkscape 0.48

3. Tips and tricks to speed up your drawing workflow

Inkscape 0.48 Essentials for Web Designers

ISBN: 978-1-84951-268-8   Paperback: 316 pages

Use the fascinating Inkscape graphics editor to create attractive layout designs, images, and icons for your website

1. The first book on the newly released Inkscape version 0.48, with an exclusive focus on web design

2. Comprehensive coverage of all aspects of Inkscape required for web design

3. Incorporate eye-catching designs, patterns, and other visual elements to spice up your web pages

Please check **www.PacktPub.com** for information on our titles

GIMP 2.6 cookbook

ISBN: 978-1-84951-202-2   Paperback: 408 pages

Over 50 recipes to produce amazing graphics with the GIMP

1. Recipes for working with the GIMP, the most powerful open source graphics package in the world

2. Straightforward instructions guide you through the tasks to unleash your true creativity without being hindered by the system

3. Part of Packt's cookbook series – practical and efficient

LaTeX Beginner's Guide

ISBN: 978-1-84719-986-7   Paperback: 336 pages

Create high-quality and professional-looking texts, articles, and books for business and science using LaTeX

1. Use LaTeX's powerful features to produce professionally designed texts

2. Install LaTeX; download, set up, and use additional styles, templates, and tools

3. Typeset math formulas and scientific expressions to the highest standards

4. Include graphics and work with figures and tables

55803186R00166

Made in the USA
Lexington, KY
07 October 2016